INTERACTI VOCABULARY NOTEBOOK

GRADES 6-8

© 2018 Erin Cobb
imlovinlit.com

Credits
Author: Erin Cobb
Proofreader: Josh Rosenberg

Carson-Dellosa Publishing LLC
PO Box 35665
Greensboro, NC 27425 USA
carsondellosa.com

Visit *carsondellosa.com* for correlations to Common Core, state, national, and Canadian provincial standards.

978-1-4838-4936-2
02-288181151

Table of Contents

Quick Notes Before You Begin . . .

1. Each template includes five vocabulary words as either tabs or separate pieces that go in a pocket. That way, students can write the definition for each word under the tab or on the back of the separate piece.

2. For each root, I have included five vocabulary words that use the root. I chose words that should be familiar (to help students make connections with the root and its meaning) as well as new words (to challenge students).

3. Each root activity also includes vocabulary cards with example words, definitions, parts of speech, and sample sentences. You might choose to have students glue these on the left-hand page opposite the template. Or, you can have students keep these in a pocket they create in the back of their notebooks.

4. In the Prefixes section, complete vocabulary cards are not included. Instead, word lists are provided for each prefix on the direction page for each activity.

5. The Suffixes section is organized into three categories: suffixes that form nouns, suffixes that form adjectives, and suffixes that form verbs and adverbs. Word lists are included on page 93.

6. This notebook can be used along with any Greek and Latin roots and affixes program. You do not have to complete all of the templates in the book—you can pick and choose the ones that you plan to cover. However, if you choose to use this book as the basis for teaching roots and affixes, refer to the Suggested Pacing Guide on page 9.

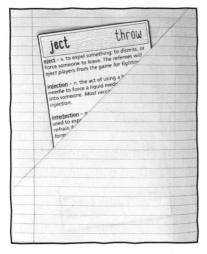

A vocabulary card is shown in the pocket in the back of a notebook.

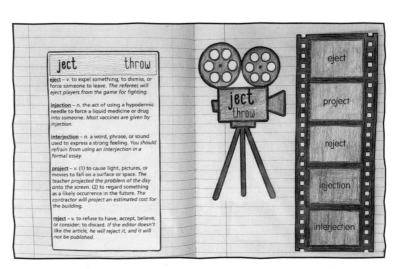

A vocabulary card is shown on the left-hand page opposite its interactive page.

Setting Up the Notebook

Wait! Don't skip! This notebook is not plug-and-play (virtually setup-free) like my others! The difference is that as we assemble this notebook, we know exactly what is going to go on each and every page. So, if you notice that the steps here are opposite of what I recommend with my other notebooks, just keep calm and notebook on! You're going to need a good hour or so to get this all set up, and remember to be patient if you're just starting to use interactive notebooks. In the explicit instructions below, I'm going to talk to you as if you're the student setting up the notebook.

1. Number the pages.
Take your brand new notebook and count off two sheets of paper starting with the first sheet in the front of the notebook. On the third sheet, write a number 1 in the top-right corner. You'll only write numbers on the right side of the notebook (never on the left side). Don't skip any pages. Number the entire notebook, leaving the last four pages blank to create a pocket (see step 3).

2. Glue in your master list.
Create a master list for the roots and affixes your class will be covering. You may choose to use the table of contents as the basis of your list (page 2) or consult your word study program. Create a document with three tables that list alphabetically all of the roots, prefixes, and suffixes, in three separate groups. Include a column for the page number each root or affix will be on. Number the pages starting at the top of the root list with *1, 2, 3*, and so on. Leave a title page at the beginning of each section; title pages will have page numbers as well (see step 4). Note that the lists are recorded alphabetically instead of in the chronological order the roots and affixes will be covered. That way, it is easier for students to refer back to specific roots as needed.

You may choose to have the roots table on a single page and the affix tables on a separate page. I prefer to glue the Prefixes/Suffixes tables onto the back of the front cover and the Roots table on the front of the first page of the notebook. You could also choose to put one on the front of the first page and one on the back of the first page.

3. Create a notebook pocket.
Create a notebook pocket with the last four pages at the end of the notebook. Glue pairs of pages together to make it sturdier. It may be helpful to refer to online video tutorials for creating pockets in interactive notebooks.

4. Create and glue in the tabs.
Refer to page 5 to see how to create and glue in the tabs for the three sections. Before you add them to the notebook, refer to your master list to see what pages they will need to fall on. For example, the Roots tab should be on page 1.

Setting Up the Notebook: Assembling Tabs

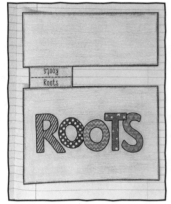

1. Color and cut out as shown.

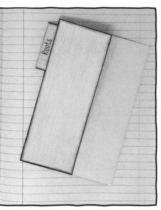

2. Fold between the "Roots" on the tab.

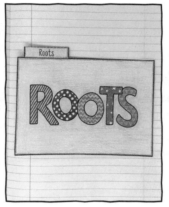

(front view)

(back view)

3. Straddle the page between the two sides.

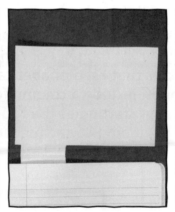

4. Lift up the front side and glue with dots.

5. Press down. Check for the white lip at top as shown.

6. Tape the inner edge.

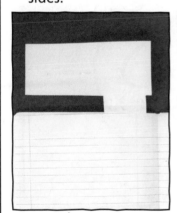

7. Turn the page and repeat with the back.

8. Tape the back crease too.

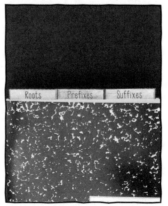

INTERACTIVE VOCABULARY NOTEBOOK
Roots Tab

Roots

Roots

Prefixes

Prefixes

PREFIXES

Suffixes

Suffixes

SUFFIXES

Suggested Pacing Guide

Unit 1

	Roots	Prefixes	Suffixes
Week 1	astr	Opposite/Against (dis-, anti-, de-, counter-, contra-)	none
Week 2	log, logue		
Week 3	circ, circum		
Week 4	mar, mer	Above/Below (hyper-, super-, hypo-, sub-)	
Week 5	grad, gres		
Week 6	mob, mot, mov		
Week 7	Review of Unit 1		

Unit 2

	Roots	Prefixes	Suffixes
Week 8	jur, jud	Greek and Latin Numbers	Noun Formers (-ance/-ence, -er/-or/-ian/-ist, -arium/-orium, -ment, -ologist/-ology, -ness, -phobia/-phobe)
Week 9	mal		
Week 10	spec		
Week 11	vit, viv	Metric Prefixes	
Week 12	man, manu		
Week 13	bene, bon		
Week 14	Review of Unit 2		

Unit 3

	Roots	Prefixes	Suffixes
Week 15	vac	Miscellaneous Set 1 (ambi-, auto-, inter-, intra-, trans-)	Adjective Formers (-able/-ible, -ish, -ic, -ive, -ous, -ly)
Week 16	mor, mort		
Week 17	frac, frag		
Week 18	hosp, host	Miscellaneous Set 2 (ab-, ad-, ex-/ef-, peri-, tele-)	
Week 19	tech		
Week 20	spir		
Week 21	Review of Unit 3		

Unit 4

	Roots	Prefixes	Suffixes
Week 22	duce, duct	Miscellaneous Set 3 (a-/an-, dys-, en-, neo-, syn-/sym-)	Verb and Adverb Formers (-ate/-ify, -en, -ize, -ward/-wise, -ly)
Week 23	voc, vok		
Week 24	foli		
Week 25	tend, tens, tent		
Week 26	Review of Unit 4		

Week 27	Review of Units 1 and 2
Week 28	Review of Units 3 and 4

Glue the center section only.

Trace the outside edges for boundaries.

Answer Key:

asterisk – *n.* a symbol (*) used in printed text, often to refer readers to a note at the bottom of the page. *The words on the page were followed by an asterisk.*

asteroid – *n.* a minor planet; one of the many small bodies circling the sun. *Most asteroids are located between the planets Mars and Jupiter.*

astronaut – *n.* a person who travels into outer space in a spacecraft. *Neil Armstrong was the first astronaut to walk on the moon.*

astronomer – *n.* a person who studies stars, planets, and other objects in outer space. *Galileo, an astronomer, discovered the first four moons of Jupiter.*

astronomical – *adj.* (1) extremely large. *The electricity bill was astronomical during December because we hung so many Christmas lights.* (2) having to do with astronomy. *The NASA scientists conducted astronomical research.*

INTERACTIVE VOCABULARY NOTEBOOK
astr - star

astr / star

asterisk – *n.* a symbol (*) used in printed text, often to refer readers to a note at the bottom of the page. *The words on the page were followed by an asterisk.*

asteroid – *n.* a minor planet; one of the many small bodies circling the sun. *Most asteroids are located between the planets Mars and Jupiter.*

astronaut – *n.* a person who travels into outer space in a spacecraft. *Neil Armstrong was the first astronaut to walk on the moon.*

astronomer – *n.* a person who studies stars, planets, and other objects in outer space. *Galileo, an astronomer, discovered the first four moons of Jupiter.*

astronomical – *adj.* (1) extremely large. *The electricity bill was astronomical during December because we hung so many Christmas lights.* (2) having to do with astronomy. *The NASA scientists conducted astronomical research.*

astr / star

asterisk – *n.* a symbol (*) used in printed text, often to refer readers to a note at the bottom of the page. *The words on the page were followed by an asterisk.*

asteroid – *n.* a minor planet; one of the many small bodies circling the sun. *Most asteroids are located between the planets Mars and Jupiter.*

astronaut – *n.* a person who travels into outer space in a spacecraft. *Neil Armstrong was the first astronaut to walk on the moon.*

astronomer – *n.* a person who studies stars, planets, and other objects in outer space. *Galileo, an astronomer, discovered the first four moons of Jupiter.*

astronomical – *adj.* (1) extremely large. *The electricity bill was astronomical during December because we hung so many Christmas lights.* (2) having to do with astronomy. *The NASA scientists conducted astronomical research.*

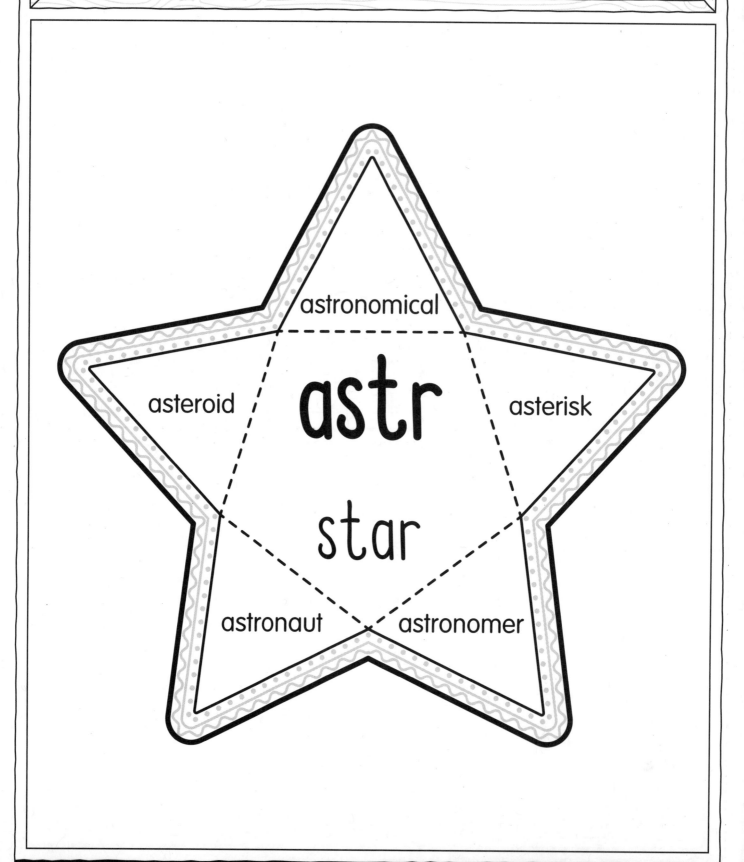

astronomical

asteroid

astr

asterisk

star

astronaut

astronomer

INTERACTIVE VOCABULARY NOTEBOOK
bene, bon - good, well

Answer Key:

beneficial – *adj.* having good or helpful consequences. *Eating fruits and vegetables is beneficial to your health.*

benevolent – *adj.* kind, generous, helpful. *The benevolent company donated millions of dollars to education.*

benign – *adj.* not causing death or serious injury; not cancerous. *Doctors removed the tumor and discovered it was benign.*

bonus – *n.* something extra, a good thing that is more than what was expected or needed. *Mrs. Miller offered two extra points as a bonus for completing the study guide.*

bountiful – *adj.* giving many enjoyable things; in large amounts. *The Pilgrims gave thanks for a bountiful harvest.*

bene, bon   good, well

beneficial – *adj.* having good or helpful consequences. *Eating fruits and vegetables is beneficial to your health.*

benevolent – *adj.* kind, generous, helpful. *The benevolent company donated millions of dollars to education.*

benign – *adj.* not causing death or serious injury; not cancerous. *Doctors removed the tumor and discovered it was benign.*

bonus – *n.* something extra, a good thing that is more than what was expected or needed. *Mrs. Miller offered two extra points as a bonus for completing the study guide.*

bountiful – *adj.* giving many enjoyable things; in large amounts. *The Pilgrims gave thanks for a bountiful harvest.*

bene, bon   good, well

beneficial – *adj.* having good or helpful consequences. *Eating fruits and vegetables is beneficial to your health.*

benevolent – *adj.* kind, generous, helpful. *The benevolent company donated millions of dollars to education.*

benign – *adj.* not causing death or serious injury; not cancerous. *Doctors removed the tumor and discovered it was benign.*

bonus – *n.* something extra, a good thing that is more than what was expected or needed. *Mrs. Miller offered two extra points as a bonus for completing the study guide.*

bountiful – *adj.* giving many enjoyable things; in large amounts. *The Pilgrims gave thanks for a bountiful harvest.*

INTERACTIVE VOCABULARY NOTEBOOK
bene, bon - good, well

bountiful

benevolent

bonus

bene, bon

good, well

beneficial

benign

INTERACTIVE VOCABULARY NOTEBOOK
circ, circum - around

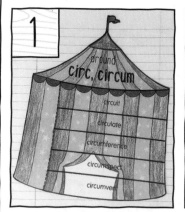

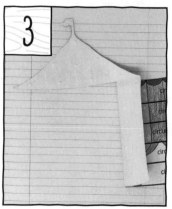

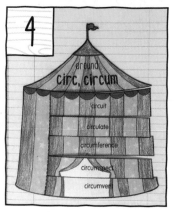

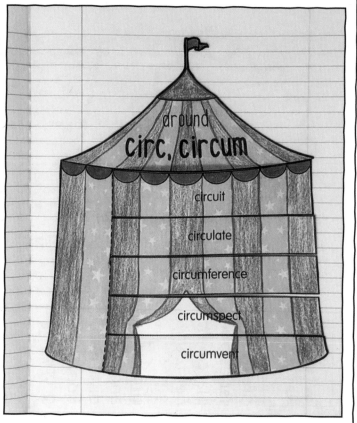

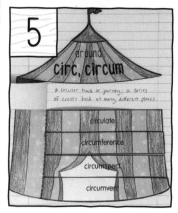

Answer Key:

circuit – *n.* a circular track or journey; a series of events held at many different places. *The pianist was relieved to complete her touring circuit.*

circulate – *v.* to go from one place to another in a circular way; to be widely distributed, as in loaned materials. *That book has been circulated among the entire group of friends.*

circumference – *n.* the length of the boundary that goes around something, particularly a circle or round area. *The circumference of my waist was definitely bigger after Thanksgiving dinner!*

circumspect – *adj.* thinking carefully about possible risks before doing or saying something; cautious. *It's wise to be circumspect, weighing the pros and cons.*

circumvent – *v.* to avoid something such as a law or rule, often dishonestly. *Lawyers often know how to circumvent the judicial system when possible.*

circ, circum around

circuit – *n.* a circular track or journey; a series of events held at many different places. *The pianist was relieved to complete her touring circuit.*

circulate – *v.* to go from one place to another in a circular way; to be widely distributed, as in loaned materials. *That book has been circulated among the entire group of friends.*

circumference – *n.* the length of the boundary that goes around something, particularly a circle or round area. *The circumference of my waist was definitely bigger after Thanksgiving dinner!*

circumspect – *adj.* thinking carefully about possible risks before doing or saying something; cautious. *It's wise to be circumspect, weighing the pros and cons.*

circumvent – *v.* to avoid something such as a law or rule, often dishonestly. *Lawyers often know how to circumvent the judicial system when possible.*

circ, circum around

circuit – *n.* a circular track or journey; a series of events held at many different places. *The pianist was relieved to complete her touring circuit.*

circulate – *v.* to go from one place to another in a circular way; to be widely distributed, as in loaned materials. *That book has been circulated among the entire group of friends.*

circumference – *n.* the length of the boundary that goes around something, particularly a circle or round area. *The circumference of my waist was definitely bigger after Thanksgiving dinner!*

circumspect – *adj.* thinking carefully about possible risks before doing or saying something; cautious. *It's wise to be circumspect, weighing the pros and cons.*

circumvent – *v.* to avoid something such as a law or rule, often dishonestly. *Lawyers often know how to circumvent the judicial system when possible.*

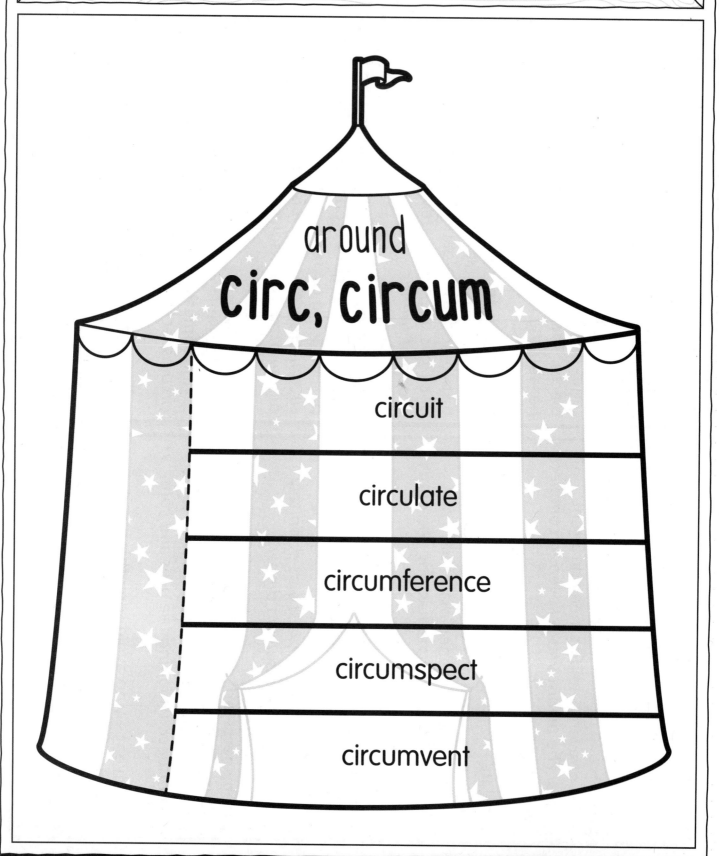

around
circ, circum

circuit

circulate

circumference

circumspect

circumvent

INTERACTIVE VOCABULARY NOTEBOOK
duce, duct - lead

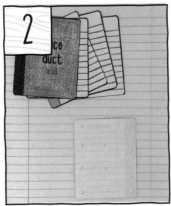

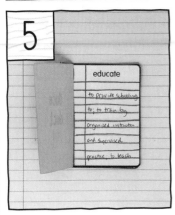

Answer Key:

deduct – *v.* to take away from a total, often an amount of money. *The shirt only costs $22 when you deduct the sale discount.*

educate – *v.* to provide schooling to; to train by organized instruction and supervised practice; to teach. *The teacher trained for years to be able to educate her students properly.*

induce – *v.* to cause someone to do something or something to happen. *Using the wrong pot could induce a grease fire.*

introduce – *v.* to present a person by name to another or a group; to bring something to first notice. *I will introduce you to my parents tonight at the party.*

produce – *v.* to make, manufacture, or bring to birth. *The factory can produce 200 boxes of cookies daily.*

duce, duct / lead

deduct – *v.* to take away from a total, often an amount of money. *The shirt only costs $22 when you deduct the sale discount.*

educate – *v.* to provide schooling to; to train by organized instruction and supervised practice; to teach. *The teacher trained for years to be able to educate her students properly.*

induce – *v.* to cause someone to do something or something to happen. *Using the wrong pot could induce a grease fire.*

introduce – *v.* to present a person by name to another or a group; to bring something to first notice. *I will introduce you to my parents tonight at the party.*

produce – *v.* to make, manufacture, or bring to birth. *The factory can produce 200 boxes of cookies daily.*

duce, duct / lead

deduct – *v.* to take away from a total, often an amount of money. *The shirt only costs $22 when you deduct the sale discount.*

educate – *v.* to provide schooling to; to train by organized instruction and supervised practice; to teach. *The teacher trained for years to be able to educate her students properly.*

induce – *v.* to cause someone to do something or something to happen. *Using the wrong pot could induce a grease fire.*

introduce – *v.* to present a person by name to another or a group; to bring something to first notice. *I will introduce you to my parents tonight at the party.*

produce – *v.* to make, manufacture, or bring to birth. *The factory can produce 200 boxes of cookies daily.*

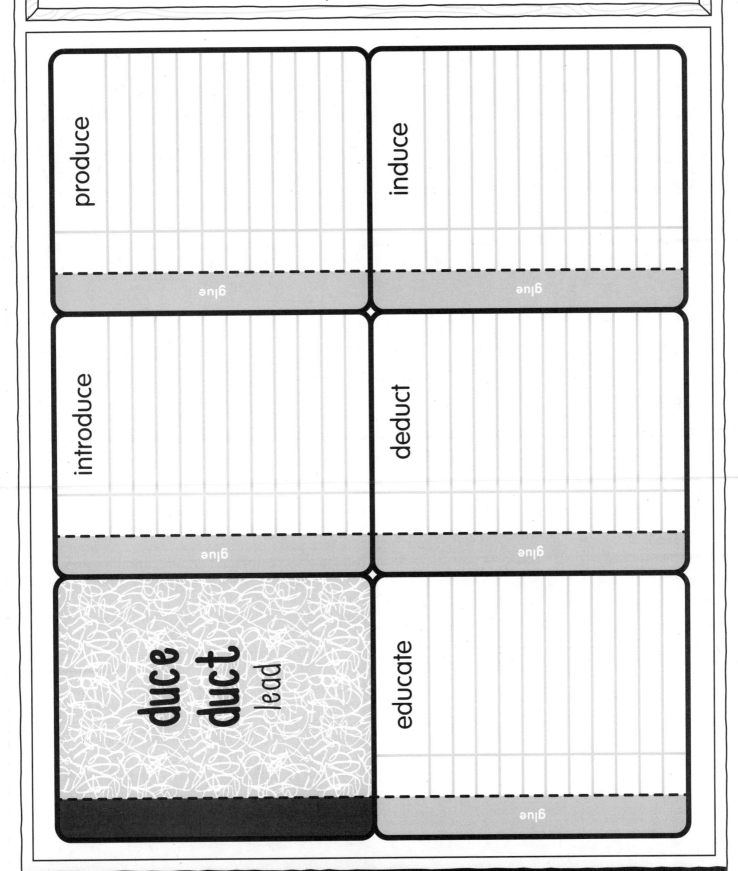

produce

induce

glue

glue

introduce

deduct

glue

glue

duce
duct
lead

educate

glue

INTERACTIVE VOCABULARY NOTEBOOK
foli - leaf

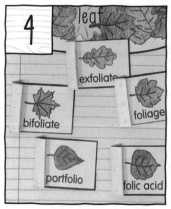

Answer Key:

bifoliate – *adj.* having exactly two leaves. *This rare bifoliate plant produces two leaves at a time.*

foliage – *n.* a combined accumulation of plant leaves. *The foliage is absolutely gorgeous in the northeast during autumn.*

folic acid – *n.* a B-complex vitamin found in leafy green vegetables that is needed to produce red blood cells. *Brussels sprouts and spinach are good sources of folic acid.*

exfoliate – *v.* to throw off, especially skin cells or scales; to peel off in thin layers. *Exfoliate your face before you use moisturizer.*

portfolio – (1) a flat case used to carry documents or drawings. *The professor set his portfolio on the table and removed his lecture notes.* (2) examples of a person's work, saved over time. *The artist offered his portfolio for consideration.*

INTERACTIVE VOCABULARY NOTEBOOK
foli - leaf

foli   leaf

bifoliate – *adj.* having exactly two leaves. *This rare bifoliate plant produces two leaves at a time.*

foliage – *n.* a combined accumulation of plant leaves. *The foliage is absolutely gorgeous in the northeast during autumn.*

folic acid – *n.* a B-complex vitamin found in leafy green vegetables that is needed to produce red blood cells. *Brussels sprouts and spinach are good sources of folic acid.*

exfoliate – *v.* to throw off, especially skin cells or scales; to peel off in thin layers. *Exfoliate your face before you use moisturizer.*

portfolio – *n.* (1) a flat case used to carry documents or drawings. *The professor set his portfolio on the table and removed his lecture notes.* (2) examples of a person's work, saved over time. *The artist offered his portfolio for consideration.*

foli   leaf

bifoliate – *adj.* having exactly two leaves. *This rare bifoliate plant produces two leaves at a time.*

foliage – *n.* a combined accumulation of plant leaves. *The foliage is absolutely gorgeous in the northeast during autumn.*

folic acid – *n.* a B-complex vitamin found in leafy green vegetables that is needed to produce red blood cells. *Brussels sprouts and spinach are good sources of folic acid.*

exfoliate – *v.* to throw off, especially skin cells or scales; to peel off in thin layers. *Exfoliate your face before you use moisturizer.*

portfolio – *n.* (1) a flat case used to carry documents or drawings. *The professor set his portfolio on the table and removed his lecture notes.* (2) examples of a person's work, saved over time. *The artist offered his portfolio for consideration.*

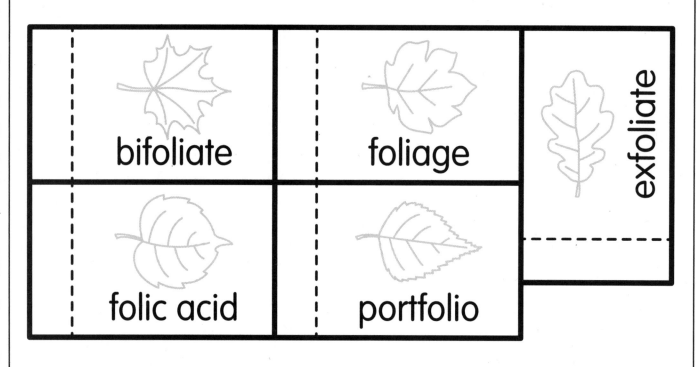

bifoliate

foliage

exfoliate

folic acid

portfolio

foli

leaf

INTERACTIVE VOCABULARY NOTEBOOK
frac, frag - to break

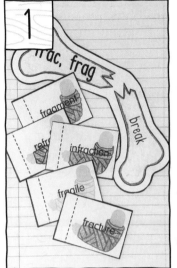

1

2

Glue the bone near the top of the page.

3

Fold the flap back on each small tab piece.

4

5

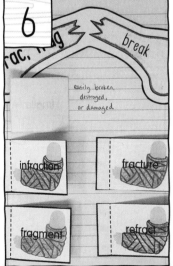

6

Answer Key:

fracture – *n.* the result of breaking something; a crack or break. *The x-ray revealed a tiny fracture in the wrist bone.*

fragile – *adj.* easily broken, destroyed, or damaged. *Be careful! The contents of the box are fragile.*

fragment – *n.* a broken part or piece of something. *Mom picked up the many fragments that used to be her favorite vase.*

infraction – *n.* an act that breaks a rule or law. *A serious infraction, such as fighting at recess, can earn you a suspension.*

refract – *v.* to make light change direction or bend as it passes through something else, such as glass. *The teacher showed how light can refract when shone through a prism.*

frac, frag   to break

fracture – *n.* the result of breaking something; a crack or break. *The x-ray revealed a tiny fracture in the wrist bone.*

fragile – *adj.* easily broken, destroyed, or damaged. *Be careful! The contents of the box are fragile.*

fragment – *n.* a broken part or piece of something. *Mom picked up the many fragments that used to be her favorite vase.*

infraction – *n.* an act that breaks a rule or law. *A serious infraction, such as fighting at recess, can earn you a suspension.*

refract – *v.* to make light change direction or bend as it passes through something else, such as glass. *The teacher showed how light can refract when shone through a prism.*

frac, frag   to break

fracture – *n.* the result of breaking something; a crack or break. *The x-ray revealed a tiny fracture in the wrist bone.*

fragile – *adj.* easily broken, destroyed, or damaged. *Be careful! The contents of the box are fragile.*

fragment – *n.* a broken part or piece of something. *Mom picked up the many fragments that used to be her favorite vase.*

infraction – *n.* an act that breaks a rule or law. *A serious infraction, such as fighting at recess, can earn you a suspension.*

refract – *v.* to make light change direction or bend as it passes through something else, such as glass. *The teacher showed how light can refract when shone through a prism.*

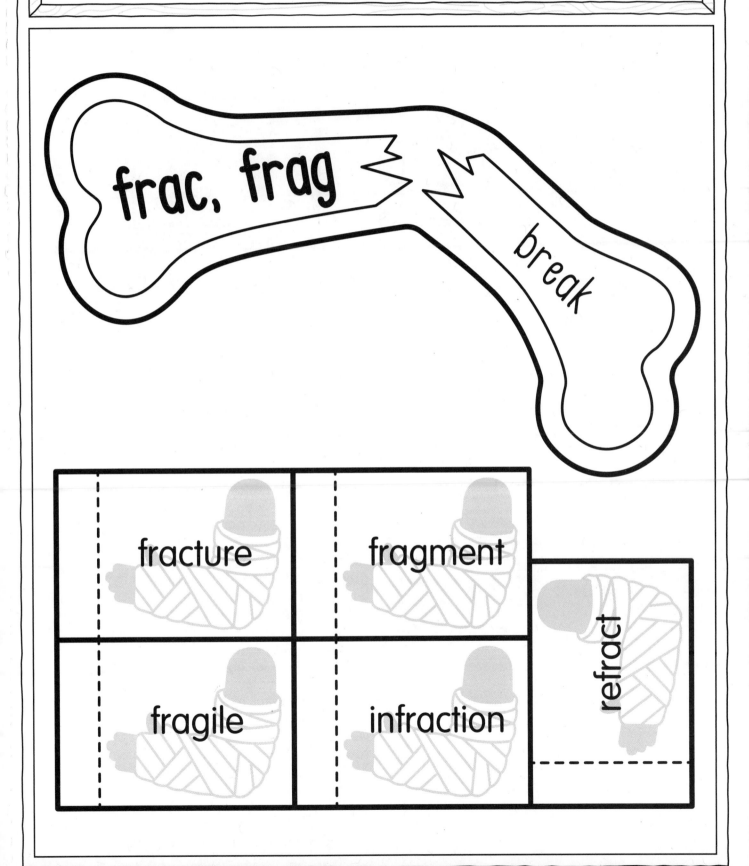

frac, frag

break

fracture

fragment

fragile

infraction

refract

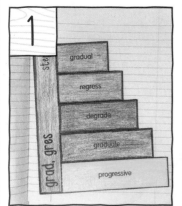

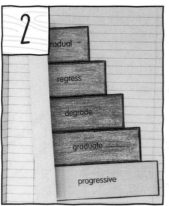

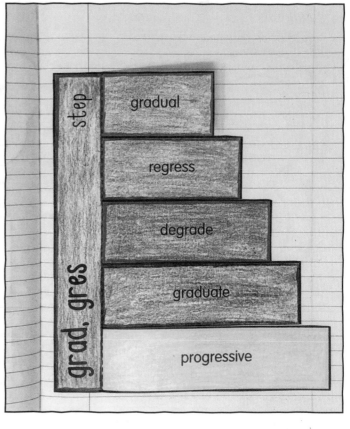

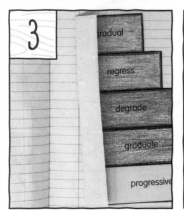

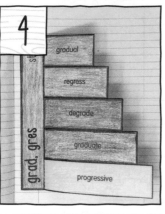

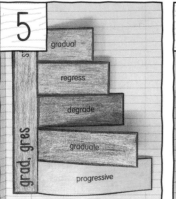

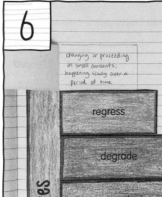

Answer Key:

degrade – *v.* (1) to treat someone poorly, without respect. *It was wrong for the teacher to degrade the student.* (2) to make the quality of something worse. *Building an oil refinery might degrade the air quality.*

gradual – *adj.* changing or proceeding in small amounts; happening slowly over a period of time. *I prefer a gradual increase in homework over a sudden increase.*

graduate – *v.* to earn a degree or diploma from a school, college, or university; to move from one level to a higher level. *Most seniors choose which college they want to attend before they graduate.*

progressive – *adj.* (1) continuing to change in stages. *The banker's progressive disease continued to worsen.* (2) using or interested in new or modern ideas. *The politician's progressive ideas excited voters.*

regress – *v.* to go backward, to return to an earlier and usually less-developed condition. *A child with autism might regress around the age of two.*

©2018 Erin Cobb • CD-105003

grad, gres / step

degrade – *v.* (1) to treat someone poorly, without respect. *It was wrong for the teacher to degrade the student.* (2) to make the quality of something worse. *Building an oil refinery might degrade the air quality.*

gradual – *adj.* changing or proceeding in small amounts; happening slowly over a period of time. *I prefer a gradual increase in homework over a sudden increase.*

graduate – *v.* to earn a degree or diploma from a school, college, or university; to move from one level to a higher level. *Most seniors choose which college they want to attend before they graduate.*

progressive – *adj.* (1) continuing to change in stages. *The banker's progressive disease continued to worsen.* (2) using or interested in new or modern ideas. *The politician's progressive ideas excited voters.*

regress – *v.* to go backward, to return to an earlier and usually less-developed condition. *A child with autism might regress around the age of two.*

grad, gres / step

degrade – *v.* (1) to treat someone poorly, without respect. *It was wrong for the teacher to degrade the student.* (2) to make the quality of something worse. *Building an oil refinery might degrade the air quality.*

gradual – *adj.* changing or proceeding in small amounts; happening slowly over a period of time. *I prefer a gradual increase in homework over a sudden increase.*

graduate – *v.* to earn a degree or diploma from a school, college, or university; to move from one level to a higher level. *Most seniors choose which college they want to attend before they graduate.*

progressive – *adj.* (1) continuing to change in stages. *The banker's progressive disease continued to worsen.* (2) using or interested in new or modern ideas. *The politician's progressive ideas excited voters.*

regress – *v.* to go backward, to return to an earlier and usually less-developed condition. *A child with autism might regress around the age of two.*

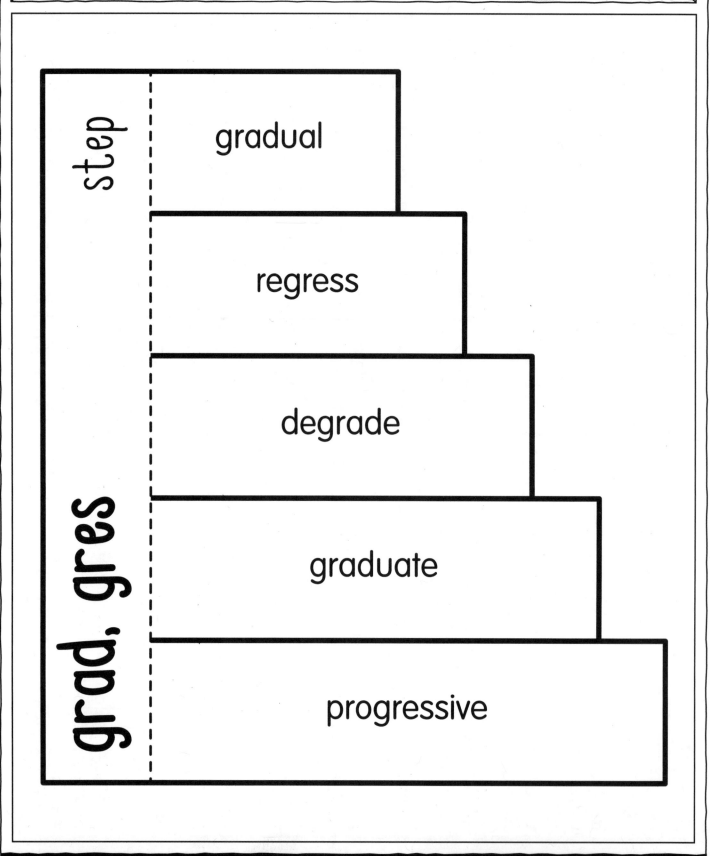

step

grad, gres

gradual

regress

degrade

graduate

progressive

INTERACTIVE VOCABULARY NOTEBOOK
hosp, host - guest, host

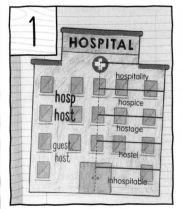

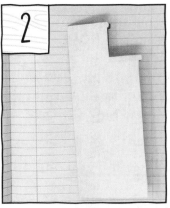

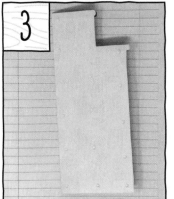

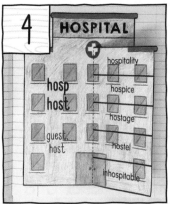

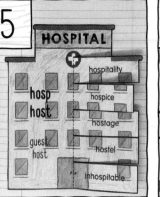

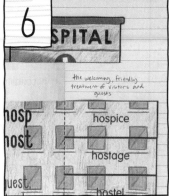

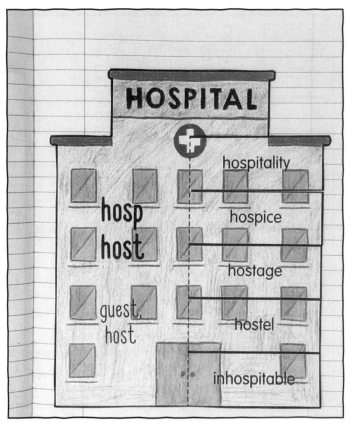

Answer Key:

hospitality – *n.* the welcoming, friendly treatment of visitors and guests. *Aunt Caren invited us over and showed us her famous hospitality.*

hospice – *n.* a place that provides for the daily and medical needs of people who are dying. *The community hospice provided a wheelchair for the dying man.*

hostage – *n.* a person who is held by someone who has made demands in exchange for freeing the person. *The bank robber took one hostage as he fled.*

hostel – *n.* an inexpensive place to sleep, usually used by young travelers. *The young couple traveled in Europe, staying in a different hostel each night.*

inhospitable – *adj.* not generous or welcoming; unfriendly to guests or visitors. *The old man was inhospitable and did not even offer us seats.*

hosp, host guest, host

hospitality – *n.* the welcoming, friendly treatment of visitors and guests. *Aunt Caren invited us over and showed us her famous hospitality.*

hospice – *n.* a place that provides for the daily and medical needs of people who are dying. *The community hospice provided a wheelchair for the dying man.*

hostage – *n.* a person who is held by someone who has made demands in exchange for freeing the person. *The bank robber took one hostage as he fled.*

hostel – *n.* an inexpensive place to sleep, usually used by young travelers. *The young couple traveled in Europe, staying in a different hostel each night.*

inhospitable – *adj.* not generous or welcoming; unfriendly to guests or visitors. *The old man was inhospitable and did not even offer us seats.*

hosp, host guest, host

hospitality – *n.* the welcoming, friendly treatment of visitors and guests. *Aunt Caren invited us over and showed us her famous hospitality.*

hospice – *n.* a place that provides for the daily and medical needs of people who are dying. *The community hospice provided a wheelchair for the dying man.*

hostage – *n.* a person who is held by someone who has made demands in exchange for freeing the person. *The bank robber took one hostage as he fled.*

hostel – *n.* an inexpensive place to sleep, usually used by young travelers. *The young couple traveled in Europe, staying in a different hostel each night.*

inhospitable – *adj.* not generous or welcoming; unfriendly to guests or visitors. *The old man was inhospitable and did not even offer us seats.*

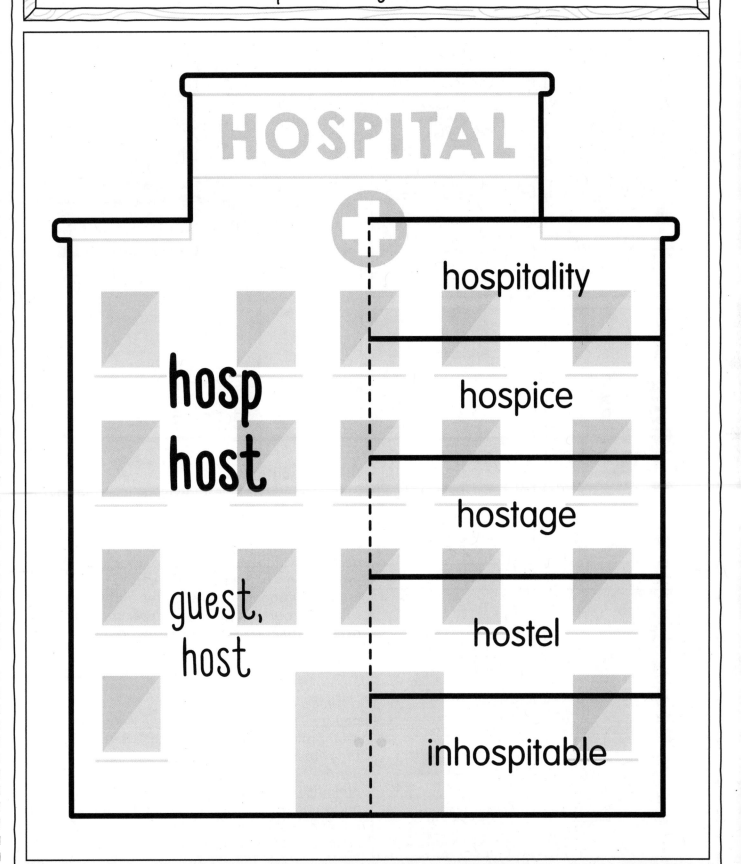

HOSPITAL

hosp
host

guest,
host

hospitality

hospice

hostage

hostel

inhospitable

INTERACTIVE VOCABULARY NOTEBOOK
jur, jud - law, justice

Glue down the top section.

Answer Key:

judgment – *n.* (1) a decision made in a court by a judge and/or jury. *The court will announce its judgment.* (2) the process of making decisions or forming opinions. *Use good judgment when deciding what is appropriate to wear to school.*

jurisdiction – *n.* the power or right to make judgments about legal issues; the authority to rule. *The court has jurisdiction over criminal offenses that occur in this county.*

juror – *n.* a member of a jury, a group chosen to hear and come to a decision in a legal case. *The juror was excused from jury duty because of his chronic illness.*

perjury – *n.* the crime of telling a lie in court after promising to tell the truth. *After she lied on the witness stand, the judge found her guilty of perjury.*

prejudice – *n.* an unfair feeling of dislike for a person or group based on their race, gender, religion, etc. *The company's history of prejudice against women is obvious.*

jur, jud law, justice

judgment – *n.* (1) a decision made in a court by a judge and/or jury. *The court will announce its judgment.* (2) the process of making decisions or forming opinions. *Use good judgment when deciding what is appropriate to wear to school.*

jurisdiction – *n.* the power or right to make judgments about legal issues; the authority to rule. *The court has jurisdiction over criminal offenses that occur in this county.*

juror – *n.* a member of a jury, a group chosen to hear and come to a decision in a legal case. *The juror was excused from jury duty because of his chronic illness.*

perjury – *n.* the crime of telling a lie in court after promising to tell the truth. *After she lied on the witness stand, the judge found her guilty of perjury.*

prejudice – *n.* an unfair feeling of dislike for a person or group based on their race, gender, religion, etc. *The company's history of prejudice against women is obvious.*

---

jur, jud law, justice

judgment – *n.* (1) a decision made in a court by a judge and/or jury. *The court will announce its judgment.* (2) the process of making decisions or forming opinions. *Use good judgment when deciding what is appropriate to wear to school.*

jurisdiction – *n.* the power or right to make judgments about legal issues; the authority to rule. *The court has jurisdiction over criminal offenses that occur in this county.*

juror – *n.* a member of a jury, a group chosen to hear and come to a decision in a legal case. *The juror was excused from jury duty because of his chronic illness.*

perjury – *n.* the crime of telling a lie in court after promising to tell the truth. *After she lied on the witness stand, the judge found her guilty of perjury.*

prejudice – *n.* an unfair feeling of dislike for a person or group based on their race, gender, religion, etc. *The company's history of prejudice against women is obvious.*

jur, jud — law, justice

judgment

juror

perjury

jurisdiction

prejudice

INTERACTIVE VOCABULARY NOTEBOOK
log, logue - word

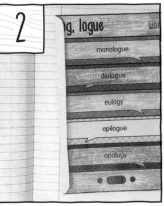

Answer Key:

apology – *n.* a statement expressing sorrow for one's actions; an expression of regret. *Kristina gave me an apology for the way she behaved at the party.*

dialogue – *n.* (1) conversation between two people. *Their dialogue was sometimes angry.* (2) lines of speech exchanged by characters in a story, movie, or play. *Find two examples of humor in the dialogue in the story.*

epilogue – *n.* a final section or speech that follows the main part of a book, play, or musical work. *The epilogue answered a lot of lingering questions.*

eulogy – *n.* a speech that praises or honors someone who has died. *The governor delivered the eulogy at the funeral.*

monologue – *n.* a long speech given by a performer or a character in a story, movie, or play. *Angela was nervous because her part in the play included a monologue that was hard to memorize.*

log, logue — word

apology – n. a statement expressing sorrow for one's actions; an expression of regret. *Kristina gave me an apology for the way she behaved at the party.*

dialogue – n. (1) conversation between two people. *Their dialogue was sometimes angry.* (2) lines of speech exchanged by characters in a story, movie, or play. *Find two examples of humor in the dialogue in the story.*

epilogue – n. a final section or speech that follows the main part of a book, play, or musical work. *The epilogue answered a lot of lingering questions.*

eulogy – n. a speech that praises or honors someone who has died. *The governor delivered the eulogy at the funeral.*

monologue – n. a long speech given by a performer or a character in a story, movie, or play. *Angela was nervous because her part in the play included a monologue that was hard to memorize.*

log, logue — word

apology – n. a statement expressing sorrow for one's actions; an expression of regret. *Kristina gave me an apology for the way she behaved at the party.*

dialogue – n. (1) conversation between two people. *Their dialogue was sometimes angry.* (2) lines of speech exchanged by characters in a story, movie, or play. *Find two examples of humor in the dialogue in the story.*

epilogue – n. a final section or speech that follows the main part of a book, play, or musical work. *The epilogue answered a lot of lingering questions.*

eulogy – n. a speech that praises or honors someone who has died. *The governor delivered the eulogy at the funeral.*

monologue – n. a long speech given by a performer or a character in a story, movie, or play. *Angela was nervous because her part in the play included a monologue that was hard to memorize.*

 imlovinlit.com ©2018 Erin Cobb • CD-105003

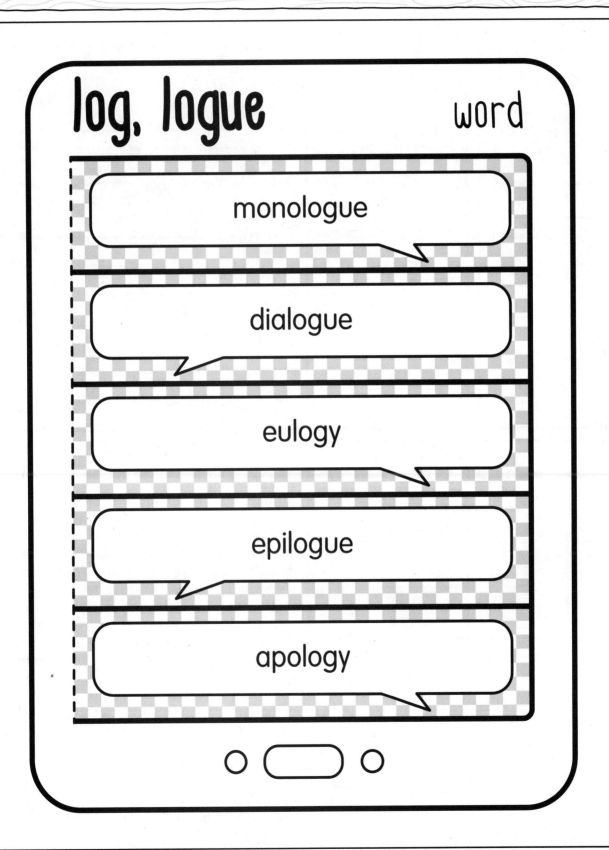

log, logue   word

- monologue
- dialogue
- eulogy
- epilogue
- apology

INTERACTIVE VOCABULARY NOTEBOOK
mal - bad, abnormal

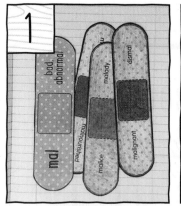

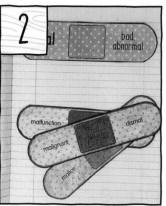

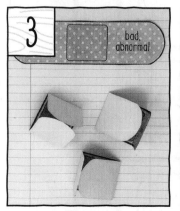

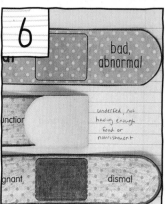

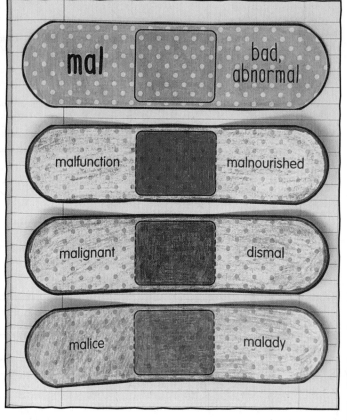

Answer Key:

dismal – *adj.* (1) gloomy or depressing. *The atmosphere during the funeral was dismal.* (2) showing a lack of skill. *He made a dismal showing during the spelling bee.*

malady – *n.* a disease or illness; *The doctor said she would fully recover from her malady.*

malfunction – *v.* to fail to function or work properly. *When a store's point-of-sale system malfunctions, no customers can be checked out.*

malice – *n.* a wish to cause harm or pain to another. *The prosecutor had to prove that the crime was committed with malice.*

malignant – *adj.* likely to grow and spread in a quick and uncontrolled way, as in a tumor; cancerous. *A biopsy can determine if a tumor is malignant and needs treatment.*

malnourished – *adj.* underfed, not having had enough food or nourishment. *In winter, some animals may become malnourished.*

©2018 Erin Cobb • CD-105003

INTERACTIVE VOCABULARY NOTEBOOK
mal - bad, abnormal

mal   bad, abnormal

dismal – *adj.* (1) gloomy or depressing. *The atmosphere during the funeral was dismal.* (2) showing a lack of skill. *He made a dismal showing during the spelling bee.*

malady – *n.* a disease or illness; *The doctor said she would fully recover from her malady.*

malfunction – *v.* to fail to function or work properly. *When a store's point-of-sale system malfunctions, no customers can be checked out.*

malice – *n.* a wish to cause harm or pain to another. *The prosecutor had to prove that the crime was committed with malice.*

malignant – *adj.* likely to grow and spread in a quick and uncontrolled way, as in a tumor; cancerous. *A biopsy can determine if a tumor is malignant and needs treatment.*

malnourished – *adj.* underfed, not having had enough food or nourishment. *In winter, some animals may become malnourished.*

mal   bad, abnormal

dismal – *adj.* (1) gloomy or depressing. *The atmosphere during the funeral was dismal.* (2) showing a lack of skill. *He made a dismal showing during the spelling bee.*

malady – *n.* a disease or illness; *The doctor said she would fully recover from her malady.*

malfunction – *v.* to fail to function or work properly. *When a store's point-of-sale system malfunctions, no customers can be checked out.*

malice – *n.* a wish to cause harm or pain to another. *The prosecutor had to prove that the crime was committed with malice.*

malignant – *adj.* likely to grow and spread in a quick and uncontrolled way, as in a tumor; cancerous. *A biopsy can determine if a tumor is malignant and needs treatment.*

malnourished – *adj.* underfed, not having had enough food or nourishment. *In winter, some animals may become malnourished.*

INTERACTIVE VOCABULARY NOTEBOOK
mal - bad, abnormal

mal   bad, abnormal

malice   malady

malignant   dismal

malfunction   malnourished

INTERACTIVE VOCABULARY NOTEBOOK
man, manu - by hand

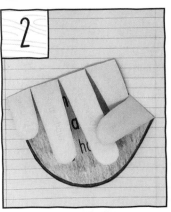

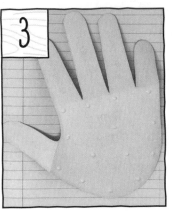

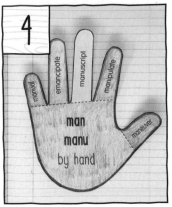

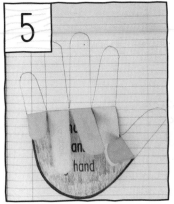

Answer Key:

emancipate – *v.* to make someone free from the control or power of another. *The teenager petitioned to become emancipated from his parents.*

manual – *adj.* (1) done by hand. *We don't have an automatic can opener, so use the manual one.* (2) *n.* a book(let) that gives instructions. *Check the manual to see how to assemble it.*

manuscript – *n.* the original copy of a play, book, piece of music, etc., usually handwritten or typed. *The writer stewed over his manuscript for hours.*

maneuver – *n.* a clever or skilled action, movement, or plan. *Dad made a scary maneuver but managed to avoid the wreck.*

manipulate – *v.* to move or control something with your hands. *We manipulated the candy pieces to look like buttons on the snowman's coat.*

man, manu — by hand

emancipate – *v.* to make someone free from the control or power of another. *The teenager petitioned to become emancipated from his parents.*

manual – *adj.* (1) done by hand. *We don't have an automatic can opener, so use the manual one.* (2) *n.* a book(let) that gives instructions. *Check the manual to see how to assemble it.*

manuscript – *n.* the original copy of a play, book, piece of music, etc., usually handwritten or typed. *The writer stewed over his manuscript for hours.*

maneuver – *n.* a clever or skilled action, movement, or plan. *Dad made a scary maneuver but managed to avoid the wreck.*

manipulate – *v.* to move or control something with your hands. *We manipulated the candy pieces to look like buttons on the snowman's coat.*

man, manu — by hand

emancipate – *v.* to make someone free from the control or power of another. *The teenager petitioned to become emancipated from his parents.*

manual – *adj.* (1) done by hand. *We don't have an automatic can opener, so use the manual one.* (2) *n.* a book(let) that gives instructions. *Check the manual to see how to assemble it.*

manuscript – *n.* the original copy of a play, book, piece of music, etc., usually handwritten or typed. *The writer stewed over his manuscript for hours.*

maneuver – *n.* a clever or skilled action, movement, or plan. *Dad made a scary maneuver but managed to avoid the wreck.*

manipulate – *v.* to move or control something with your hands. *We manipulated the candy pieces to look like buttons on the snowman's coat.*

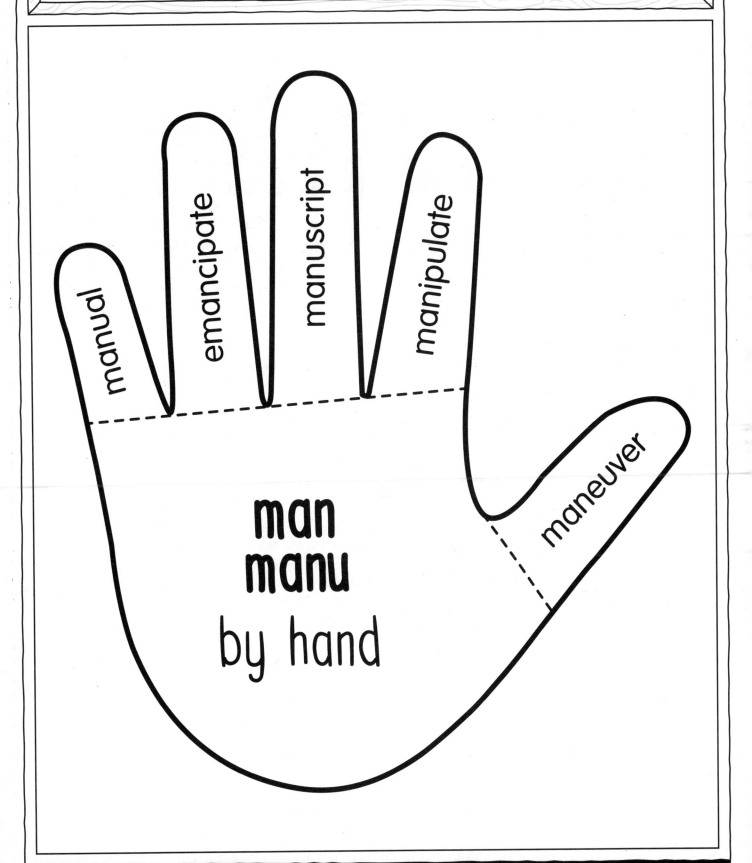

INTERACTIVE VOCABULARY NOTEBOOK
mar, mer - sea, pool

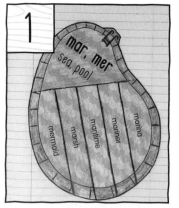

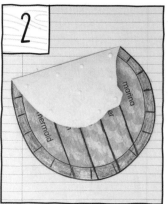

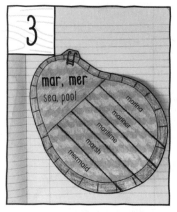

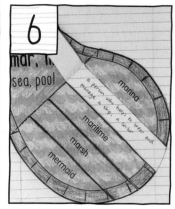

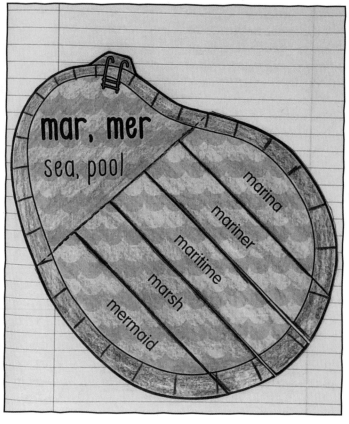

Answer Key:

marina – *n.* a specially designed area of water where privately owned boats are kept. *Jake idled the boat closer to the marina and tied it up.*

mariner – *n.* a person who helps to steer and manage a ship; a sailor. *The mariner was thrilled to have a few days off, on land!*

maritime – *adj.* having to do with the sea. *The king ordered maritime explorations off of the coast of Portugal.*

marsh – *n.* an area of soft, wet land where grasses and other plants grow. *Watch out, there are many mosquitoes near the marsh!*

mermaid – *n.* an imaginary sea creature that is said to have a woman's head and body but a fish's tail for legs. *The mermaid longed to be a human and to live on land.*

INTERACTIVE VOCABULARY NOTEBOOK

mar, mer - sea, pool

mar, mer — sea, pool

marina – *n.* a specially designed area of water where privately owned boats are kept. *Jake idled the boat closer to the marina and tied it up.*

mariner – *n.* a person who helps to steer and manage a ship; a sailor. *The mariner was thrilled to have a few days off, on land!*

maritime – *adj.* having to do with the sea. *The king ordered maritime explorations off of the coast of Portugal.*

marsh – *n.* an area of soft, wet land where grasses and other plants grow. *Watch out, there are many mosquitoes near the marsh!*

mermaid – *n.* an imaginary sea creature that is said to have a woman's head and body but a fish's tail for legs. *The mermaid longed to be a human and to live on land.*

mar, mer — sea, pool

marina – *n.* a specially designed area of water where privately owned boats are kept. *Jake idled the boat closer to the marina and tied it up.*

mariner – *n.* a person who helps to steer and manage a ship; a sailor. *The mariner was thrilled to have a few days off, on land!*

maritime – *adj.* having to do with the sea. *The king ordered maritime explorations off of the coast of Portugal.*

marsh – *n.* an area of soft, wet land where grasses and other plants grow. *Watch out, there are many mosquitoes near the marsh!*

mermaid – *n.* an imaginary sea creature that is said to have a woman's head and body but a fish's tail for legs. *The mermaid longed to be a human and to live on land.*

mar, mer

sea, pool

marina

mariner

maritime

marsh

mermaid

INTERACTIVE VOCABULARY NOTEBOOK
mob, mot, mov - move

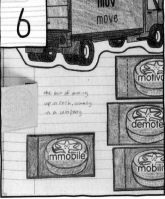

Answer Key:

demote – *v.* to lower the rank or position of someone to a less important one. *The boss may demote you for poor job performance.*

immobile – *adj.* unable to move. *The car sat immobile due to a flat tire.*

mobility – *n.* the ability to move or to be mobile. *A wheelchair can greatly improve mobility for someone with a disability.*

motivate – *v.* to give someone a good reason to do something. *Coach sure knows how to motivate us to be on time for practice!*

promotion – *n.* the act of moving up in rank, usually in a company. *Mom is hoping to get a promotion and a raise at work.*

INTERACTIVE VOCABULARY NOTEBOOK
mob, mot, mov - move

mob, mot, mov move

demote – v. to lower the rank or position of someone to a less important one. *The boss may demote you for poor job performance.*

immobile – adj. unable to move. *The car sat immobile due to a flat tire.*

mobility – n. the ability to move or to be mobile. *A wheelchair can greatly improve mobility for someone with a disability.*

motivate – v. to give someone a good reason to do something. *Coach sure knows how to motivate us to be on time for practice!*

promotion – n. the act of moving up in rank, usually in a company. *Mom is hoping to get a promotion and a raise at work.*

mob, mot, mov move

demote – v. to lower the rank or position of someone to a less important one. *The boss may demote you for poor job performance.*

immobile – adj. unable to move. *The car sat immobile due to a flat tire.*

mobility – n. the ability to move or to be mobile. *A wheelchair can greatly improve mobility for someone with a disability.*

motivate – v. to give someone a good reason to do something. *Coach sure knows how to motivate us to be on time for practice!*

promotion – n. the act of moving up in rank, usually in a company. *Mom is hoping to get a promotion and a raise at work.*

imlovinlit.com
©2018 Erin Cobb • CD-105003

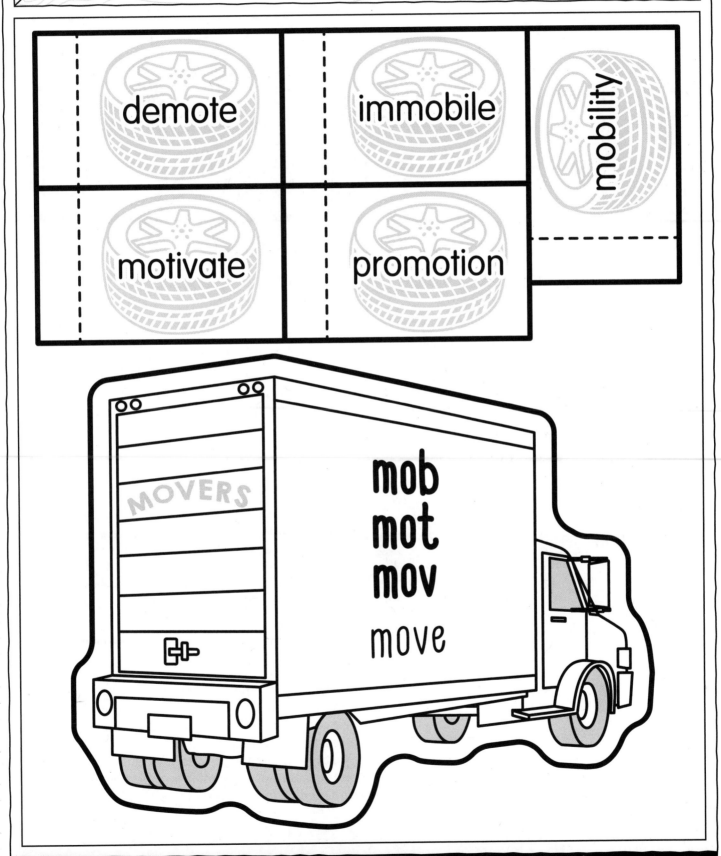

demote

immobile

mobility

motivate

promotion

mob
mot
mov
move

MOVERS

INTERACTIVE VOCABULARY NOTEBOOK
mor, mort - death

Answer Key:

immortal – *adj.* able to live forever. *According to folklore, some creatures are immortal.*

morgue – *n.* a place where the bodies of dead people are kept for a time pending identification or discovery of cause of death. *The elderly gentleman was taken to the morgue after his death.*

mortality – *n.* the deaths of numerous people or animals. *The mortality rates are higher for people in less developed nations.*

mortician – *n.* a person whose job is to prepare dead people's bodies for burial; a funeral director. *The curious child wants to learn about becoming a mortician someday.*

mortify – *v.* to cause or feel extreme embarrassment or humiliation. *To be sent to the principal's office would mortify me!*

mor, mort   death

immortal – *adj.* able to live forever.
According to folklore, some creatures are immortal.

morgue – *n.* a place where the bodies of dead people are kept for a time pending identification or discovery of cause of death. *The elderly gentleman was taken to the morgue after his death.*

mortality – *n.* the deaths of numerous people or animals. *The mortality rates are higher for people in less developed nations.*

mortician – *n.* a person whose job is to prepare dead people's bodies for burial; a funeral director. *The curious child wants to learn about becoming a mortician someday.*

mortify – *v.* to cause or feel extreme embarrassment or humiliation. *To be sent to the principal's office would mortify me!*

mor, mort   death

immortal – *adj.* able to live forever.
According to folklore, some creatures are immortal.

morgue – *n.* a place where the bodies of dead people are kept for a time pending identification or discovery of cause of death. *The elderly gentleman was taken to the morgue after his death.*

mortality – *n.* the deaths of numerous people or animals. *The mortality rates are higher for people in less developed nations.*

mortician – *n.* a person whose job is to prepare dead people's bodies for burial; a funeral director. *The curious child wants to learn about becoming a mortician someday.*

mortify – *v.* to cause or feel extreme embarrassment or humiliation. *To be sent to the principal's office would mortify me!*

INTERACTIVE VOCABULARY NOTEBOOK
mor, mort - death

immortal

mortality

mortician

morgue

mortify

mor
mort

death

INTERACTIVE VOCABULARY NOTEBOOK
spec - look, see

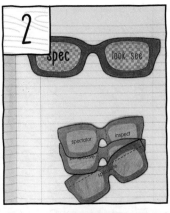

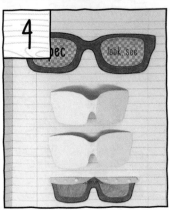

Answer Key:

inspect – *v.* to look something over carefully; to officially visit a facility to check if rules and/or laws are being followed. *The principal inspected students' lockers today.*

perspective – *n.* (1) a personal way of thinking about or understanding issues or ideas. *Molly asked for Jim's perspective on the reasons for going to war.* (2) the way a scene is visible from near to far. *The perspective in the painting is wrong, making the house look lopsided.*

prospect – *n.* the possibility that something will happen in the future. *The prospect of losing electrical power is real.*

spectator – *n.* a person who watches an event, show, game, or activity, sometimes as part of an audience. *Hundreds of spectators waited for the parade to begin.*

speculate – *v.* to consider something and make guesses about it; to form ideas or theories about an unknown. *It's interesting to speculate about what the criminal was thinking.*

INTERACTIVE VOCABULARY NOTEBOOK
spec - look, see

spec | look, see

inspect – *v.* to look something over carefully; to officially visit a facility to check if rules and/or laws are being followed. *The principal inspected students' lockers today.*

perspective – *n.* (1) a personal way of thinking about or understanding issues or ideas. *Molly asked for Jim's perspective on the reasons for going to war.* (2) the way a scene is visible from near to far. *The perspective in the painting is wrong, making the house look lopsided.*

prospect – *n.* the possibility that something will happen in the future. *The prospect of losing electrical power is real.*

spectator – *n.* a person who watches an event, show, game, or activity, sometimes as part of an audience. *Hundreds of spectators waited for the parade to begin.*

speculate – *v.* to consider something and make guesses about it; to form ideas or theories about an unknown. *It's interesting to speculate about what the criminal was thinking.*

spec | look, see

inspect – *v.* to look something over carefully; to officially visit a facility to check if rules and/or laws are being followed. *The principal inspected students' lockers today.*

perspective – *n.* (1) a personal way of thinking about or understanding issues or ideas. *Molly asked for Jim's perspective on the reasons for going to war.* (2) the way a scene is visible from near to far. *The perspective in the painting is wrong, making the house look lopsided.*

prospect – *n.* the possibility that something will happen in the future. *The prospect of losing electrical power is real.*

spectator – *n.* a person who watches an event, show, game, or activity, sometimes as part of an audience. *Hundreds of spectators waited for the parade to begin.*

speculate – *v.* to consider something and make guesses about it; to form ideas or theories about an unknown. *It's interesting to speculate about what the criminal was thinking.*

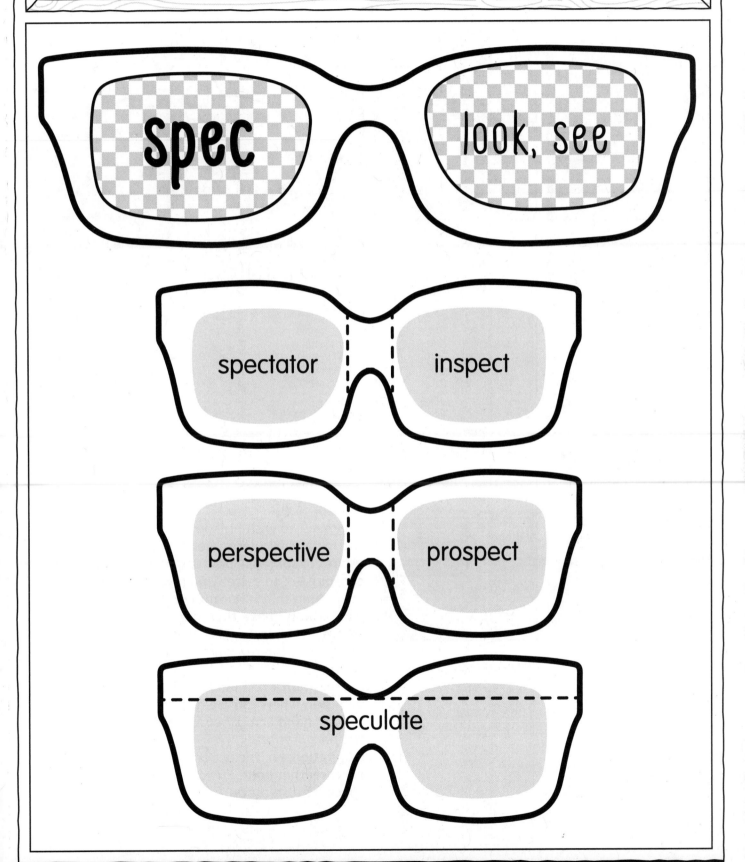

spec

look, see

spectator

inspect

perspective

prospect

speculate

imlovinlit.com

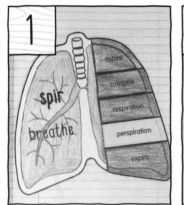

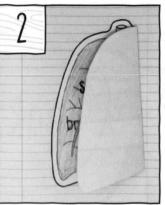

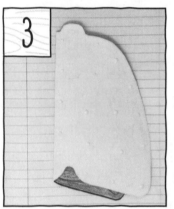

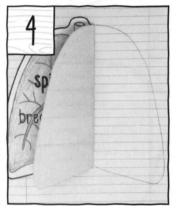

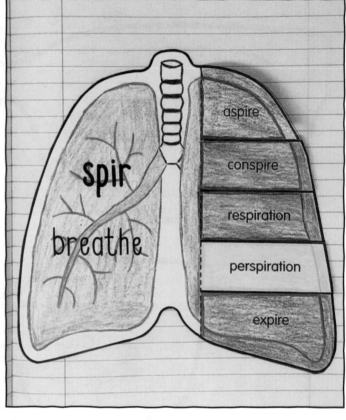

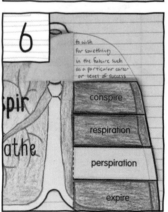

Answer Key:

aspire – *v.* to wish for something in the future such as a particular career or level of success. *He aspires to someday be a commercial airline pilot.*

conspire – *v.* to secretly plan with someone to do something that is harmful or illegal. *Two prisoners conspired to make their big escape.*

expire – *v.* to end or die; to no longer be valid. *The milk in the refrigerator doesn't expire until Friday.*

perspiration – *n.* a salty, clear liquid that forms on your skin when you are hot or nervous; sweat. *She ran her hand across her forehead and wiped off the perspiration.*

respiration – *n.* the act or process of breathing in and breathing out. *The doctor will be in shortly to check his respiration.*

spir | breathe

aspire – *v.* to wish for something in the future such as a particular career or level of success. *He aspires to someday be a commercial airline pilot.*

conspire – *v.* to secretly plan with someone to do something that is harmful or illegal. *Two prisoners conspired to make their big escape.*

expire – *v.* to end or die; to no longer be valid. *The milk in the refrigerator doesn't expire until Friday.*

perspiration – *n.* a salty, clear liquid that forms on your skin when you are hot or nervous; sweat. *She ran her hand across her forehead and wiped off the perspiration.*

respiration – *n.* the act or process of breathing in and breathing out. *The doctor will be in shortly to check his respiration.*

spir | breathe

aspire – *v.* to wish for something in the future such as a particular career or level of success. *He aspires to someday be a commercial airline pilot.*

conspire – *v.* to secretly plan with someone to do something that is harmful or illegal. *Two prisoners conspired to make their big escape.*

expire – *v.* to end or die; to no longer be valid. *The milk in the refrigerator doesn't expire until Friday.*

perspiration – *n.* a salty, clear liquid that forms on your skin when you are hot or nervous; sweat. *She ran her hand across her forehead and wiped off the perspiration.*

respiration – *n.* the act or process of breathing in and breathing out. *The doctor will be in shortly to check his respiration.*

INTERACTIVE VOCABULARY NOTEBOOK
spir - breathe

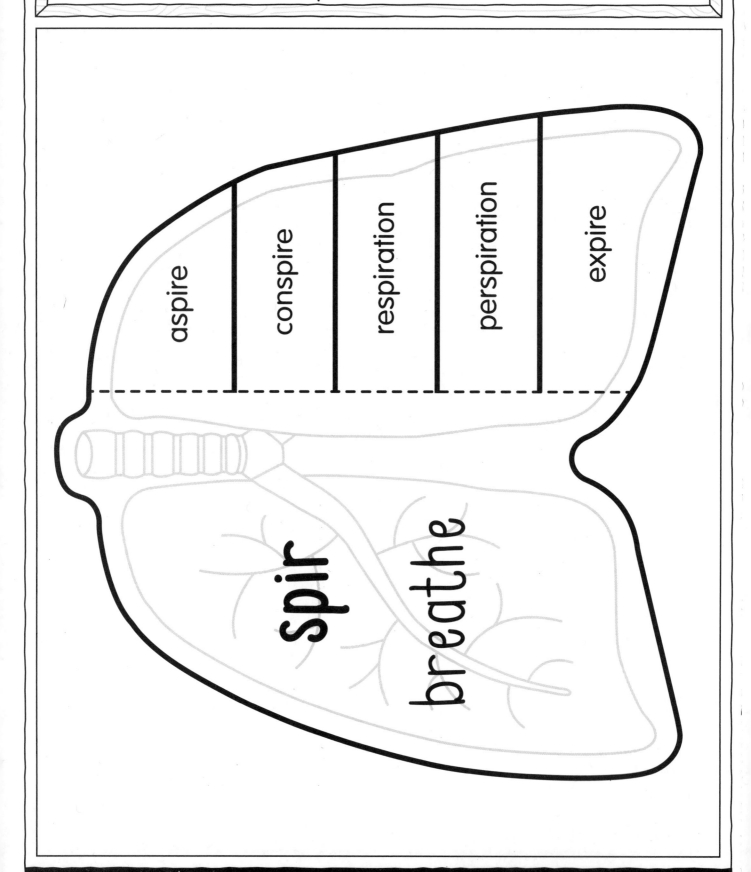

aspire

conspire

respiration

perspiration

expire

spir

breathe

imlovinlit.com

INTERACTIVE VOCABULARY NOTEBOOK
tech - skill, art

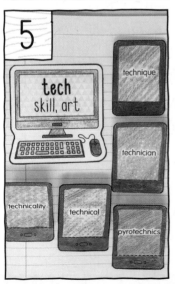

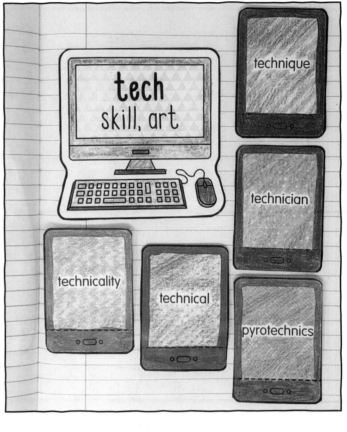

Answer Key:

pyrotechnics – *n.* a bright display of fireworks. *We enjoyed watching the pyrotechnics on the last night of our vacation.*

technical – *adj.* having to do with a specific field of art, science, or industry. *When Dad talks about work, the vocabulary he uses is too technical for me.*

technicality – *n.* a small detail in a rule, law, etc., especially one that can bring about an unexpected result. *Tenia was disqualified from the spelling bee due to a technicality.*

technician – *n.* a person who is a specialist in a field of science, industry, medicine, etc. *The computer technician finally arrived to fix my laptop.*

technique – *n.* a particular way of doing something by using a special knowledge or skill. *I wish I could master my grandmother's technique of making the perfect pie crust.*

INTERACTIVE VOCABULARY NOTEBOOK
tech - skill, art

tech   skill, art

pyrotechnics – *n.* a bright display of fireworks. *We enjoyed watching the pyrotechnics on the last night of our vacation.*

technical – *adj.* having to do with a specific field of art, science, or industry. *When Dad talks about work, the vocabulary he uses is too technical for me.*

technicality – *n.* a small detail in a rule, law, etc., especially one that can bring about an unexpected result. *Tenia was disqualified from the spelling bee due to a technicality.*

technician – *n.* a person who is a specialist in a field of science, industry, medicine, etc. *The computer technician finally arrived to fix my laptop.*

technique – *n.* a particular way of doing something by using a special knowledge or skill. *I wish I could master my grandmother's technique of making the perfect pie crust.*

tech   skill, art

pyrotechnics – *n.* a bright display of fireworks. *We enjoyed watching the pyrotechnics on the last night of our vacation.*

technical – *adj.* having to do with a specific field of art, science, or industry. *When Dad talks about work, the vocabulary he uses is too technical for me.*

technicality – *n.* a small detail in a rule, law, etc., especially one that can bring about an unexpected result. *Tenia was disqualified from the spelling bee due to a technicality.*

technician – *n.* a person who is a specialist in a field of science, industry, medicine, etc. *The computer technician finally arrived to fix my laptop.*

technique – *n.* a particular way of doing something by using a special knowledge or skill. *I wish I could master my grandmother's technique of making the perfect pie crust.*

INTERACTIVE VOCABULARY NOTEBOOK
tech - skill, art

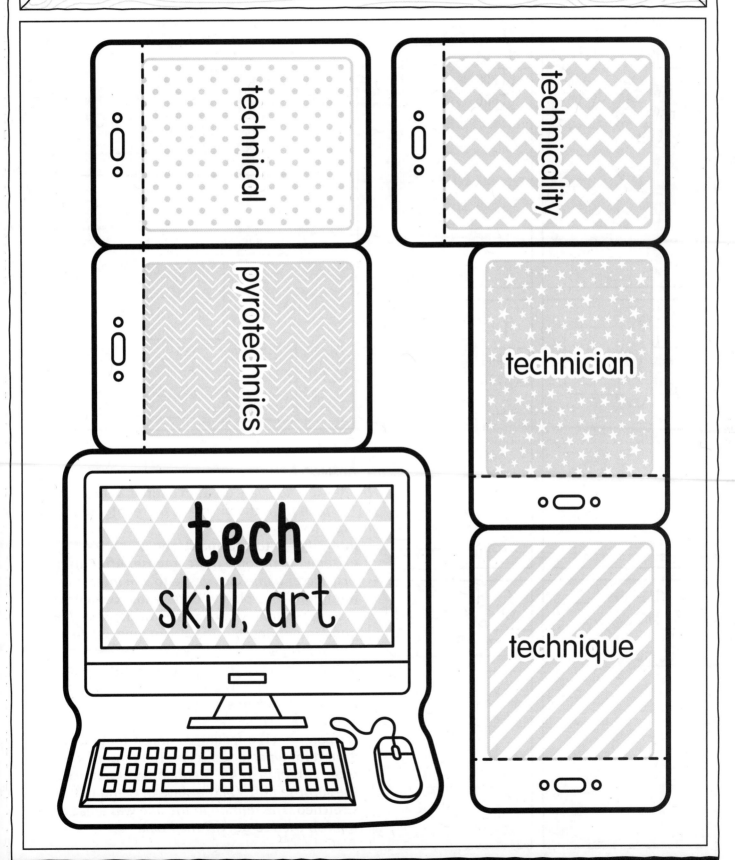

technical

technicality

pyrotechnics

technician

tech
skill, art

technique

INTERACTIVE VOCABULARY NOTEBOOK
tend, tens, tent - stretch, strain

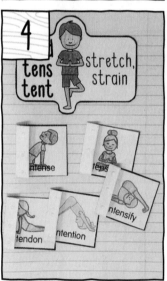

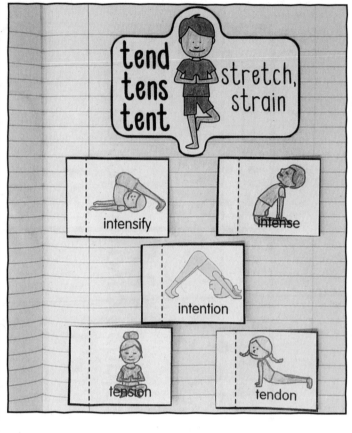

Answer Key:

intense – *adj.* very great in degree; very strong. *The pain from the burn was more intense than he expected.*

intensify – *v.* to become stronger or more extreme; to become more intense. *After losing her first soccer game, her desire to win intensified.*

intention – *n.* a plan to behave in a certain way or accomplish something; an aim or purpose. *I had good intentions, but they went awry when I ran out of money.*

tendon – *n.* a tough cord of tissue that connects a muscle to a bone. *The Achilles tendon is a band of tissue that connects the calf muscles to the heel bone.*

tension – *n.* (1) a feeling of unrest that makes it hard for a person to relax. *The tension in the room was high as Mr. Stephenson announced the surprise quiz.* (2) the state of being tightly stretched. *The tension in the line was amazing as the fish tried to get off the hook.*

tend, tens, tent — stretch, strain

intense – *adj.* very great in degree; very strong. *The pain from the burn was more intense than he expected.*

intensify – *v.* to become stronger or more extreme; to become more intense. *After losing her first soccer game, her desire to win intensified.*

intention – *n.* a plan to behave in a certain way or accomplish something; an aim or purpose. *I had good intentions, but they went awry when I ran out of money.*

tendon – *n.* a tough cord of tissue that connects a muscle to a bone. *The Achilles tendon is a band of tissue that connects the calf muscles to the heel bone.*

tension – *n.* (1) a feeling of unrest that makes it hard for a person to relax. *The tension in the room was high as Mr. Stephenson announced the surprise quiz.* (2) the state of being tightly stretched. *The tension in the line was amazing as the fish tried to get off the hook.*

tend, tens, tent — stretch, strain

intense – *adj.* very great in degree; very strong. *The pain from the burn was more intense than he expected.*

intensify – *v.* to become stronger or more extreme; to become more intense. *After losing her first soccer game, her desire to win intensified.*

intention – *n.* a plan to behave in a certain way or accomplish something; an aim or purpose. *I had good intentions, but they went awry when I ran out of money.*

tendon – *n.* a tough cord of tissue that connects a muscle to a bone. *The Achilles tendon is a band of tissue that connects the calf muscles to the heel bone.*

tension – *n.* (1) a feeling of unrest that makes it hard for a person to relax. *The tension in the room was high as Mr. Stephenson announced the surprise quiz.* (2) the state of being tightly stretched. *The tension in the line was amazing as the fish tried to get off the hook.*

tend
tens
tent

stretch,
strain

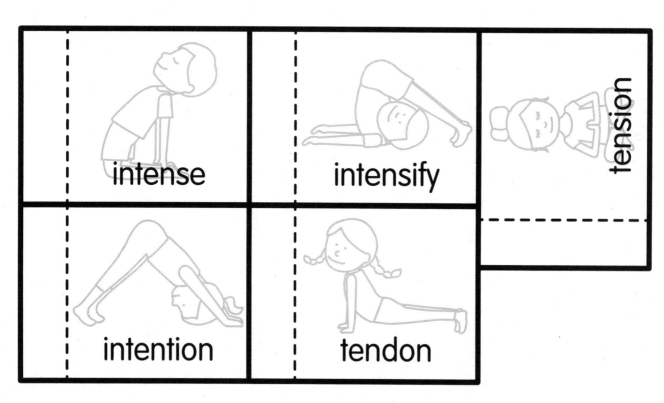

intense

intensify

tension

intention

tendon

INTERACTIVE VOCABULARY NOTEBOOK
vac - empty, free

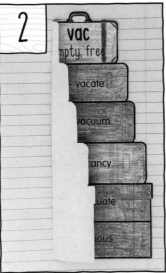

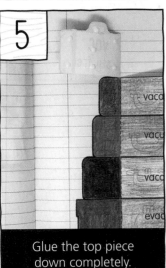

Glue the top piece down completely.

Answer Key:

evacuate – *v.* to remove people from a situation of danger; to leave a dangerous place. *The mayor advised the citizens to evacuate ahead of the storm.*

vacate – *v.* to leave a job or position; to give up a seat, hotel room, etc. *College students are required to vacate the dormitory within one week of the last day of the semester.*

vacancy – *n.* a job or position in a company that is available; a room or space that is not occupied. *The front desk clerk told us that there was only one vacancy at the hotel.*

vacuous – *adj.* having or showing a lack of depth of thought; with little if any meaning, importance, or substance. *The man's silly and vacuous complaint went nowhere.*

vacuum – *n.* an empty space in which there is no air or other matter; a space from which all or most matter has been removed. *The scientist created a vacuum in a glass container.*

imlovinlit.com

vac — empty, free

evacuate – *v.* to remove people from a situation of danger; to leave a dangerous place. *The mayor advised the citizens to evacuate ahead of the storm.*

vacate – *v.* to leave a job or position; to give up a seat, hotel room, etc. *College students are required to vacate the dormitory within one week of the last day of the semester.*

vacancy – *n.* a job or position in a company that is available; a room or space that is not occupied. *The front desk clerk told us that there was only one vacancy at the hotel.*

vacuous – *adj.* having or showing a lack of depth of thought; with little if any meaning, importance, or substance. *The man's silly and vacuous complaint went nowhere.*

vacuum – *n.* an empty space in which there is no air or other matter; a space from which all or most matter has been removed. *The scientist created a vacuum in a glass container.*

vac — empty, free

evacuate – *v.* to remove people from a situation of danger; to leave a dangerous place. *The mayor advised the citizens to evacuate ahead of the storm.*

vacate – *v.* to leave a job or position; to give up a seat, hotel room, etc. *College students are required to vacate the dormitory within one week of the last day of the semester.*

vacancy – *n.* a job or position in a company that is available; a room or space that is not occupied. *The front desk clerk told us that there was only one vacancy at the hotel.*

vacuous – *adj.* having or showing a lack of depth of thought; with little if any meaning, importance, or substance. *The man's silly and vacuous complaint went nowhere.*

vacuum – *n.* an empty space in which there is no air or other matter; a space from which all or most matter has been removed. *The scientist created a vacuum in a glass container.*

INTERACTIVE VOCABULARY NOTEBOOK
vac - empty, free

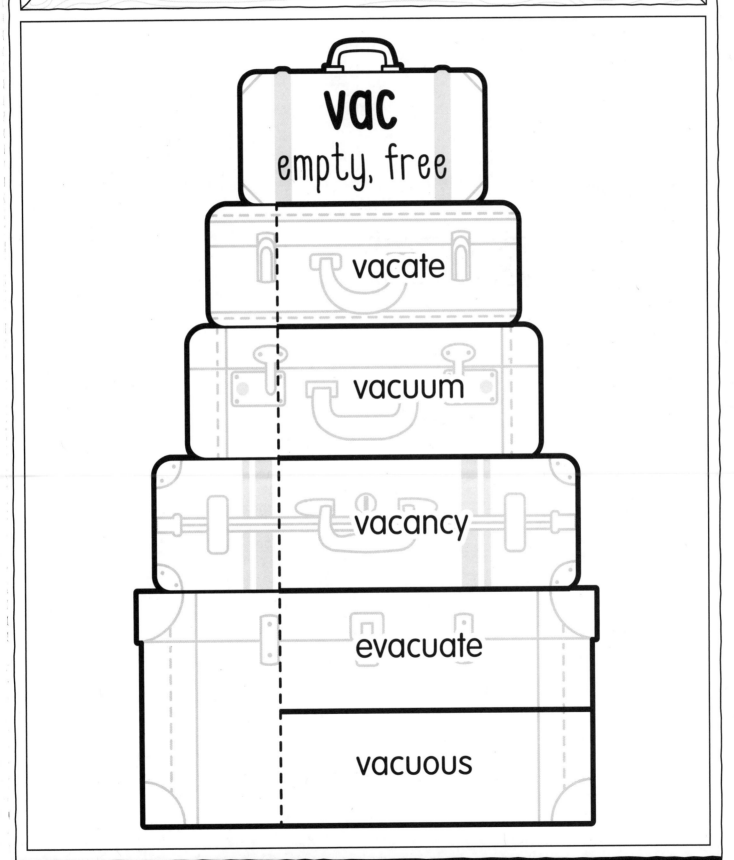

vac
empty, free

vacate

vacuum

vacancy

evacuate

vacuous

imlovinlit.com

INTERACTIVE VOCABULARY NOTEBOOK
vit, viv - life, alive

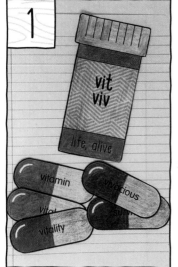

Glue the sides and bottom only to make a pocket.

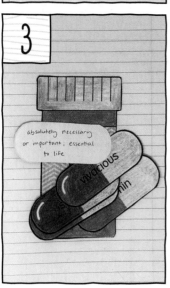

Answer Key:

survival – *n.* the state of continuing to live or exist, especially despite and through difficult conditions. *The probability of survival is higher than ever for cancer patients.*

vitality – *n.* an inner force of power and strength; the power or ability to live and grow. *Regular exercise will improve your vitality.*

vital – *adj.* absolutely necessary or important; essential to life. *The nurse played a vital role in the man's recovery.*

vitamin – *n.* a natural substance found in small amounts in foods and bodies that contributes to health; a pill containing vitamins. *Many breakfast cereals are fortified with vitamins.*

vivacious – *adj.* happy and lively in spirit and actions. *The contestant's vivacious personality shone through and was reflected in the judges' scores.*

vit, viv   life, alive

survival – *n.* the state of continuing to live or exist, especially despite and through difficult conditions. *The probability of survival is higher than ever for cancer patients.*

vitality – *n.* an inner force of power and strength; the power or ability to live and grow. *Regular exercise will improve your vitality.*

vital – *adj.* absolutely necessary or important; essential to life. *The nurse played a vital role in the man's recovery.*

vitamin – *n.* a natural substance found in small amounts in foods and bodies that contributes to health; a pill containing vitamins. *Many breakfast cereals are fortified with vitamins.*

vivacious – *adj.* happy and lively in spirit and actions. *The contestant's vivacious personality shone through and was reflected in the judges' scores.*

vit, viv   life, alive

survival – *n.* the state of continuing to live or exist, especially despite and through difficult conditions. *The probability of survival is higher than ever for cancer patients.*

vitality – *n.* an inner force of power and strength; the power or ability to live and grow. *Regular exercise will improve your vitality.*

vital – *adj.* absolutely necessary or important; essential to life. *The nurse played a vital role in the man's recovery.*

vitamin – *n.* a natural substance found in small amounts in foods and bodies that contributes to health; a pill containing vitamins. *Many breakfast cereals are fortified with vitamins.*

vivacious – *adj.* happy and lively in spirit and actions. *The contestant's vivacious personality shone through and was reflected in the judges' scores.*

imlovinlit.com

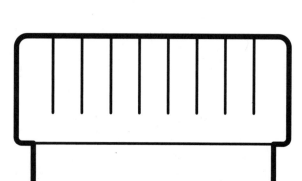

vitamin

vital

vivacious

survival

vitality

INTERACTIVE VOCABULARY NOTEBOOK
voc, vok - voice, call

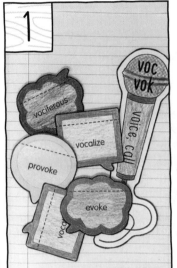

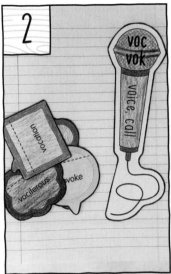

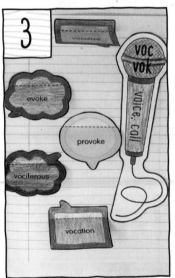

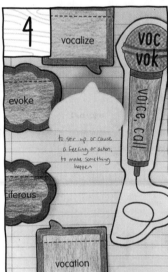

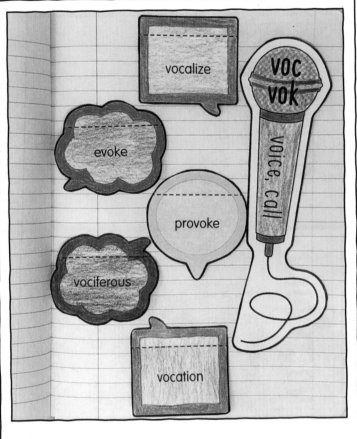

Answer Key:

evoke – *v.* to bring a memory, feeling, or image to mind. *The dreary winter season can sometimes evoke sadness.*

provoke – *v.* to stir up or cause a feeling or action; to make something happen. *If you provoke a fight, you are as guilty as those who are fighting.*

vocalize – *v.* to express something with the voice, such as speech or song. *Mom spoke with the manager to vocalize her discontent with the service.*

vocation – *n.* a specific occupation or profession; a calling to spend your life doing a certain kind of work. *It's best to know what vocation you'd like to pursue before finishing high school.*

vociferous – *adj.* making a very loud and emphatic sound. *The toddler was quite vociferous when she didn't get her way.*

INTERACTIVE VOCABULARY NOTEBOOK
voc, vok – voice, call

voc, vok voice, call

evoke – *v.* to bring a memory, feeling, or image to mind. *The dreary winter season can sometimes evoke sadness.*

provoke – *v.* to stir up or cause a feeling or action; to make something happen. *If you provoke a fight, you are as guilty as those who are fighting.*

vocalize – *v.* to express something with the voice, such as speech or song. *Mom spoke with the manager to vocalize her discontent with the service.*

vocation – *n.* a specific occupation or profession; a calling to spend your life doing a certain kind of work. *It's best to know what vocation you'd like to pursue before finishing high school.*

vociferous – *adj.* making a very loud and emphatic sound. *The toddler was quite vociferous when she didn't get her way.*

voc, vok voice, call

evoke – *v.* to bring a memory, feeling, or image to mind. *The dreary winter season can sometimes evoke sadness.*

provoke – *v.* to stir up or cause a feeling or action; to make something happen. *If you provoke a fight, you are as guilty as those who are fighting.*

vocalize – *v.* to express something with the voice, such as speech or song. *Mom spoke with the manager to vocalize her discontent with the service.*

vocation – *n.* a specific occupation or profession; a calling to spend your life doing a certain kind of work. *It's best to know what vocation you'd like to pursue before finishing high school.*

vociferous – *adj.* making a very loud and emphatic sound. *The toddler was quite vociferous when she didn't get her way.*

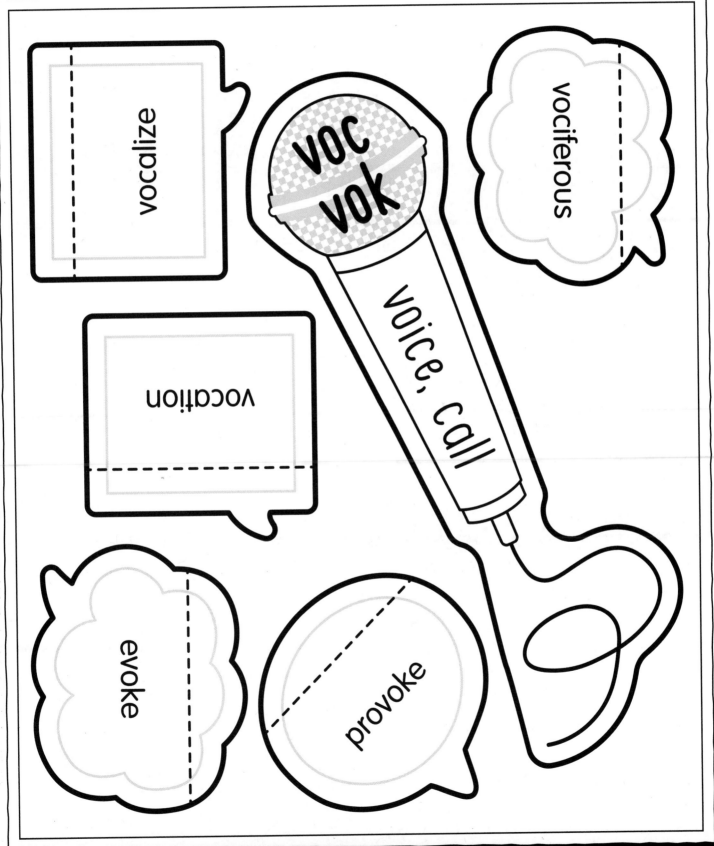

voc vok

voice, call

vocalize

vociferous

vocation

evoke

provoke

INTERACTIVE VOCABULARY NOTEBOOK
Greek & Latin Numbers

1

Color and cut out the pieces of the template. It's much easier to write on the pieces before gluing, so consider doing that now if students will be recording examples or other information.

2

Glue in the bottom section only. Use tiny baby dots so that gluing all 10 together doesn't make the paper wet. Start with 10 and go all the way to one.

3

Fold the bottom of the cover up.

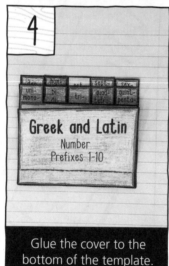

4

Glue the cover to the bottom of the template.

*HINT: This will be a thick page in the notebook, so glue this notebook page and the notebook page that follows together to make it extra sturdy.

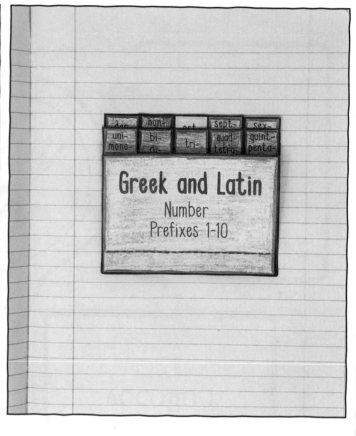

Answer Key
Latin/Greek Number Prefixes

uni-/mono- (one) – unicorn, monopoly, monologue

bi-/di- (two) – billion, bicycle, dialogue, dilemma

tri-/tri- (three) – triathlon, triangle, trio, trilogy

quad-/tetra- (four) – quadrant, quartet, tetragram

quint-/penta- (five) – quintet, quintuple, pentagon

sex-/hex- (six) – sextant, sextet, hexagon

sept-/hept- (seven) – septuplet, heptagon

oct-/oct- (eight) – octet, octave, octopus

non-/ennea- (nine) – nonillion, enneangle

dec-/dec- (ten) – decade, decathlon, decagon

INTERACTIVE VOCABULARY NOTEBOOK
Greek & Latin Numbers

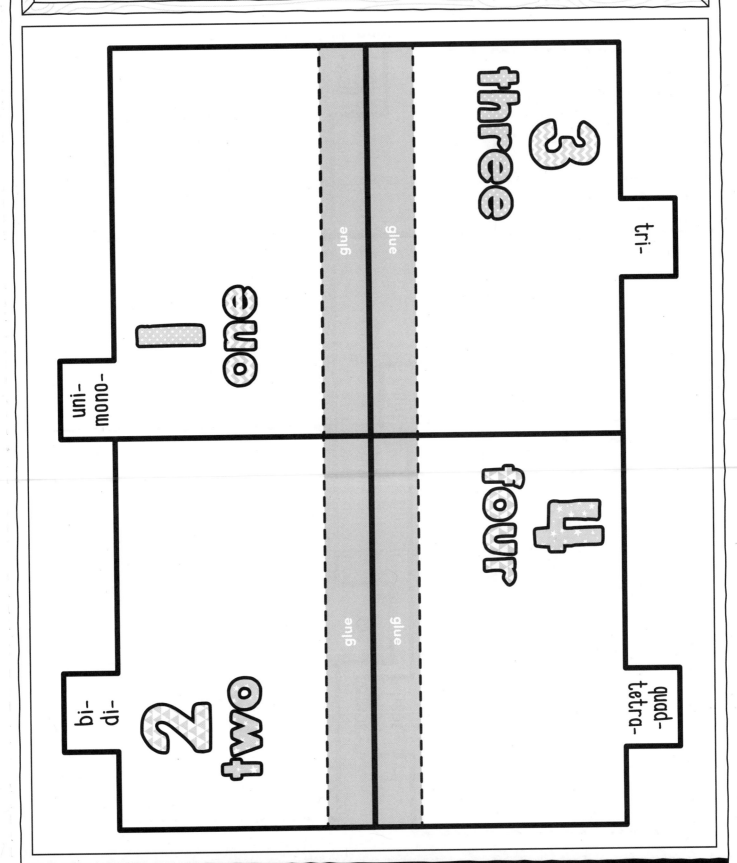

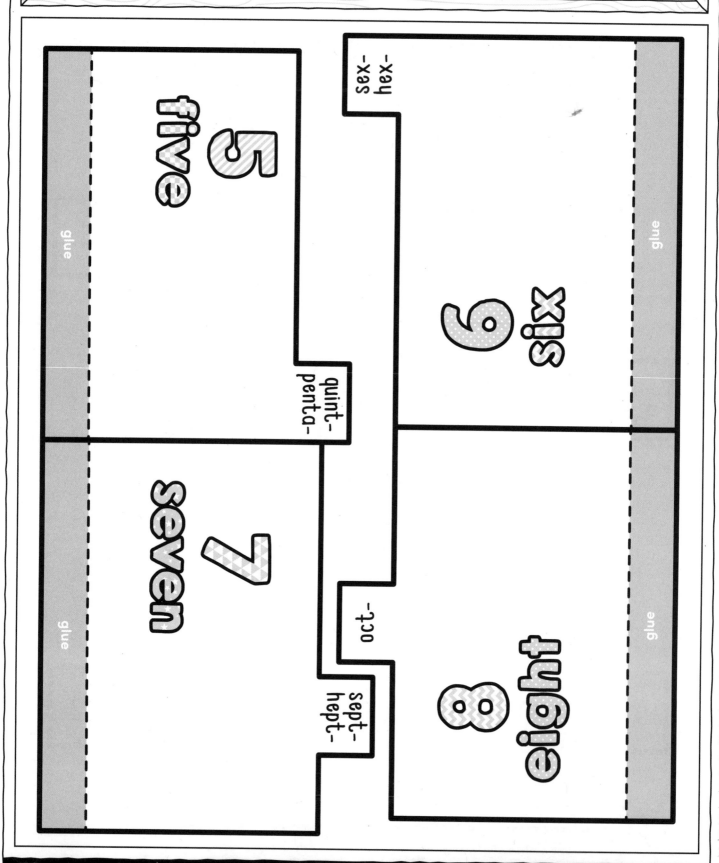

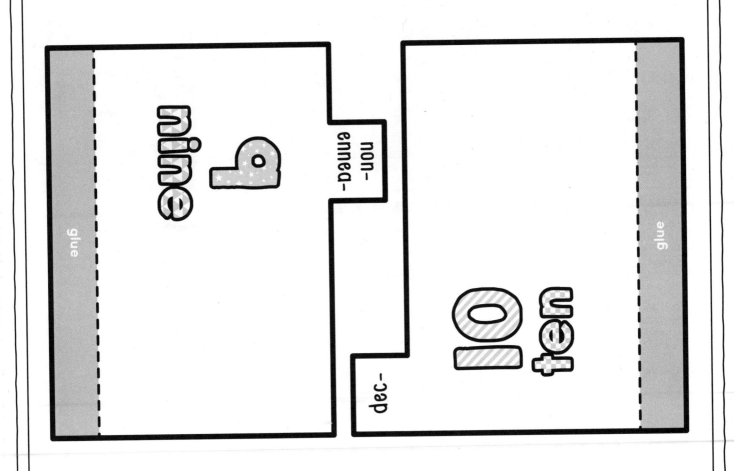

Greek and Latin
Number
Prefixes 1-10

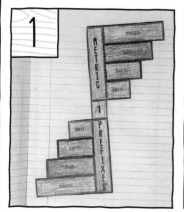

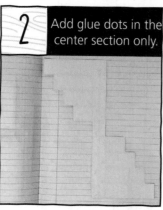

Add glue dots in the center section only.

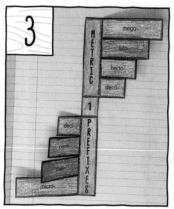

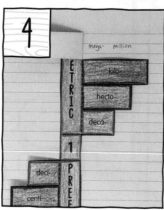

Answer Key:
Metric System Prefixes
<u>mega-</u> million
<u>kilo-</u> thousand
<u>hecto-</u> hundred
<u>deca-</u> ten
<u>deci-</u> tenth
<u>centi-</u> hundredth
<u>milli-</u> thousandth
<u>micro-</u> millionth

Metric System Base Units
<u>linear measurement</u> – meters
<u>weight measurement</u> – grams
<u>volume measurement</u> – liters
<u>time measurement</u> – seconds
<u>power measurement</u> – watts

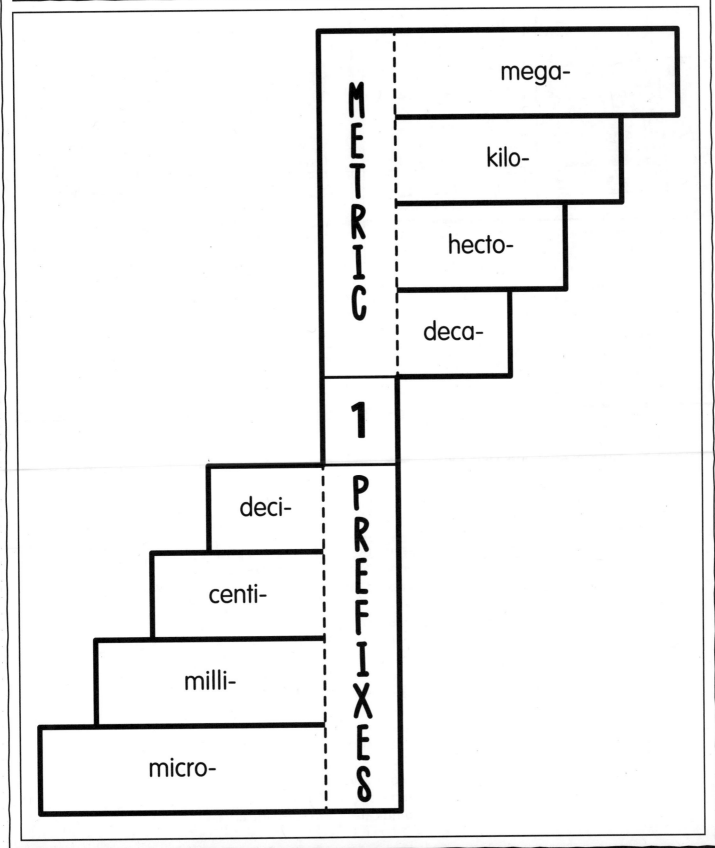

INTERACTIVE VOCABULARY NOTEBOOK
Prefixes: opposite, against

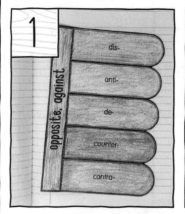
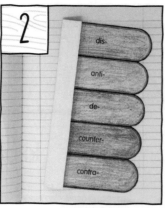
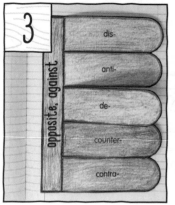
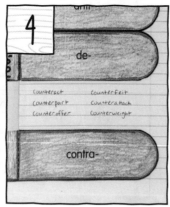

Answer Key:

<u>dis-</u> (not, opposite of) – disapprove, discover, distrust, dishonest, disappear, disconnect, displace, disgrace, disloyal, disable

<u>anti-</u> (against) – antibiotic, antidote, antiseptic, antisocial, antislavery, antipathy, antibacterial, antitrust, antidepressant, antiracist

<u>de-</u> (opposite from, away) – decode, decrease, deduct, deject, decline, depress, deport, depart, deprive, destructive

<u>counter-</u> (opposite) – counterfeit, counteract, counterargument, counterassault, counterattack, counteroffer, counteroffensive, counterpart, counterweight, countersuit

<u>contra-</u> (against) – contradict, contradiction, contract, contraction, contrast, contrasting, contravene, contraindicate, contrary, contrarious

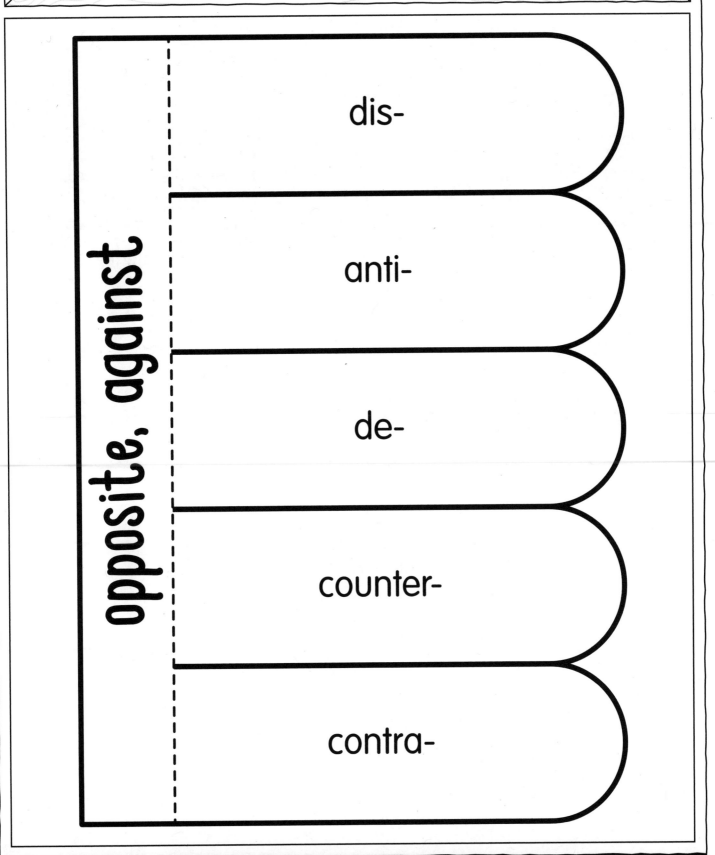

opposite, against

dis-

anti-

de-

counter-

contra-

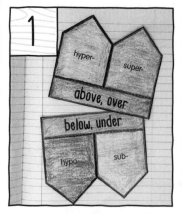

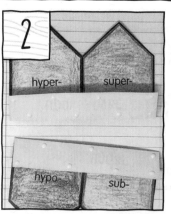

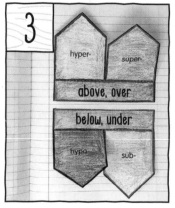

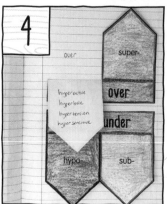

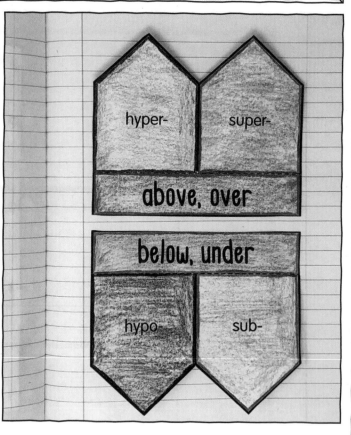

Answer Key:

<u>hyper-</u> (over) – hyperactive, hyperbole, hypertension, hypersensitive, hyperplasia

<u>super-</u> (above) – supervise, superintendent, superior, supernatural, superimpose

<u>hypo-</u> (under) – hypothermia, hypoallergenic, hypothesis, hypothetical, hypocrite

<u>sub-</u> (below) – subway, subpar, subscribe, subside, subconscious

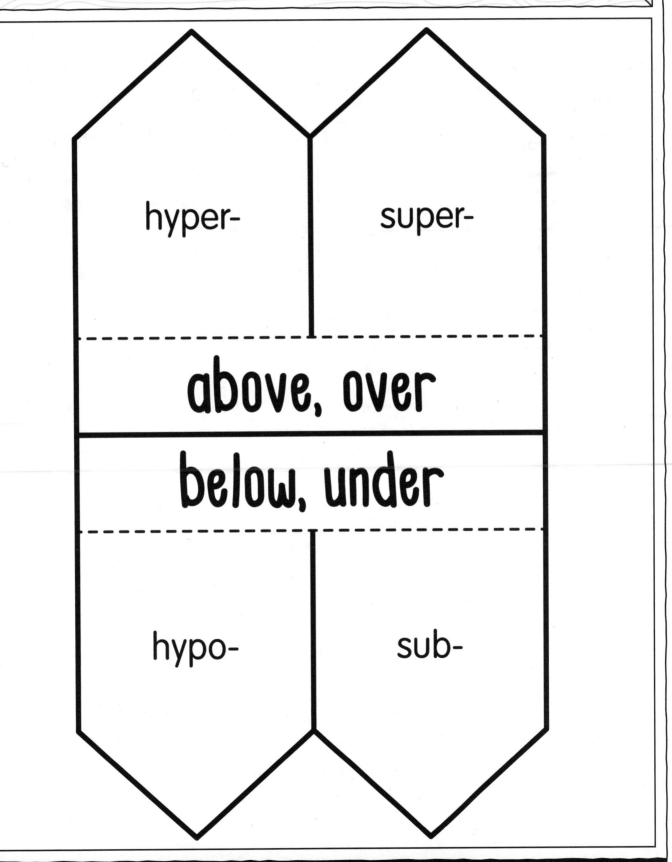

hyper-

super-

above, over

below, under

hypo-

sub-

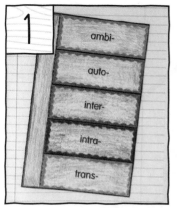
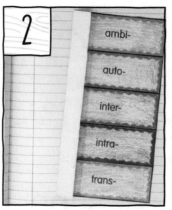
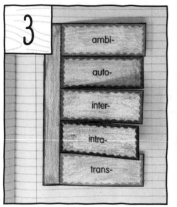
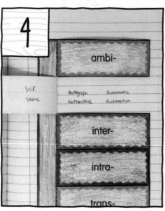
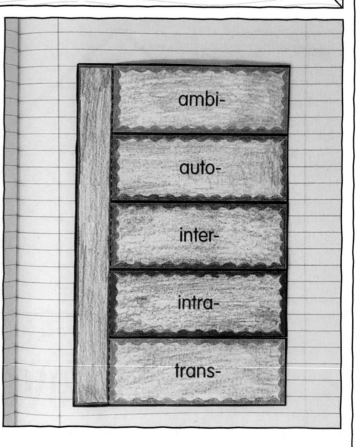

Answer Key:

ambi- (both, two) – ambidextrous, ambivalent, ambiguous, ambiguity, ambivert

auto- (self, same) – autograph, automation, automobile, automatic, autonomy

inter- (between, among) – international, interfere, interim, interval, interrupt

intra- (inside, within) – intranet, intravenous, intracellular, intrapersonal, intrapopulation

trans- (across, beyond, change) – translate, transmit, transport, transform, transition

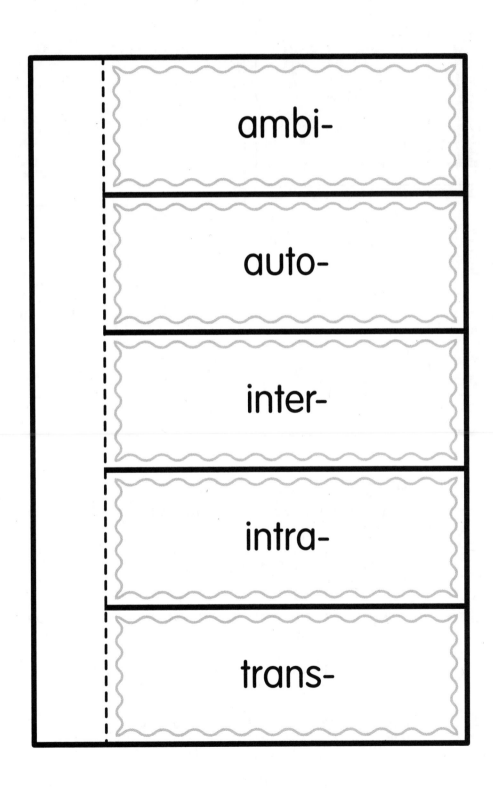

ambi-

auto-

inter-

intra-

trans-

INTERACTIVE VOCABULARY NOTEBOOK
Prefixes: Miscellaneous Set 2

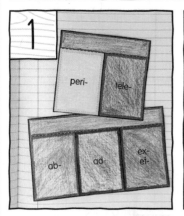

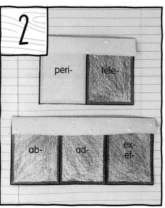

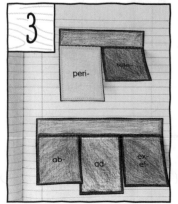

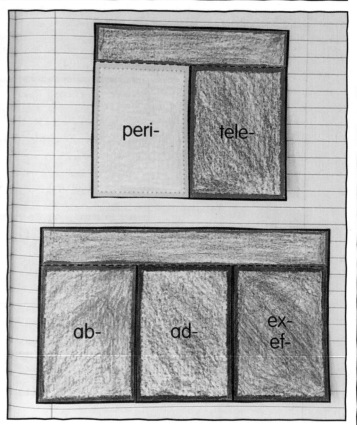

Answer Key:

ab- (away from) – absent, abdicate, abstain, abnormal, abuse

ad- (to, toward) – advance, addict, adjunct, adjacent, admire

ex-/ef- (out, away from) – export, expansion, express, exit, effluent

peri- (around) – perimeter, periscope, peripheral, periodontal, periphrasis

tele- (far) – televise, telescope, telepathic, telegraph, televangelist

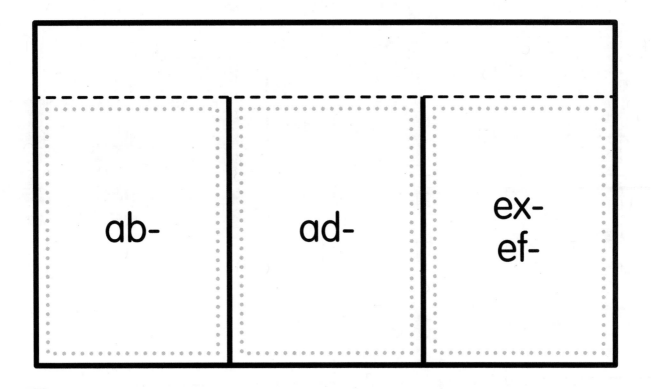

ab-   ad-   ex-
              ef-

peri-   tele-

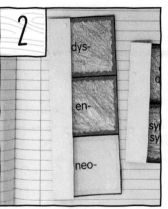

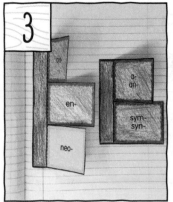

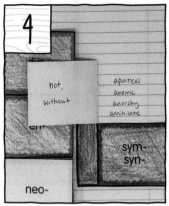

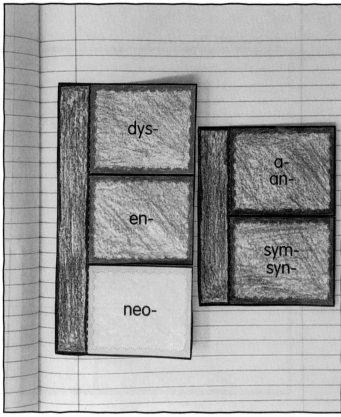

Answer Key:

<u>a-/an-</u> (not, without) – atheist, apolitical, anemic, anarchy, annihilate

<u>dys-</u> (bad, abnormal) – dysfunction, dyslexia, dysentery, dystrophy, dyspepsia

<u>en-</u> (cause to) – enforce, enlighten, entitle, encourage, enjoy

<u>neo-</u> (new) – neonatal, neon, neoclassical, neoprene, neonatologist

<u>syn-/sym-</u> (with, together) – symphony, sympathy, symbolic, synonymous, synthesis

©2018 Erin Cobb • CD-105003

INTERACTIVE VOCABULARY NOTEBOOK

Prefixes: Miscellaneous Set 3

dys-

en-

neo-

a-
an-

sym-
syn-

INTERACTIVE VOCABULARY NOTEBOOK
Suffixes

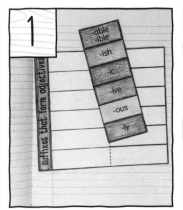

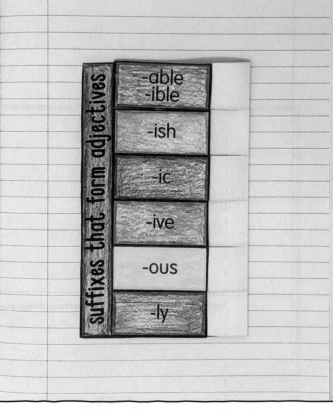

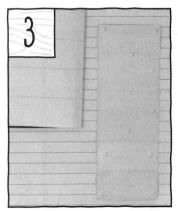

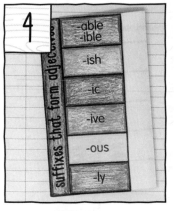

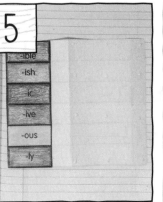

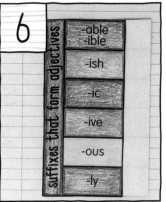

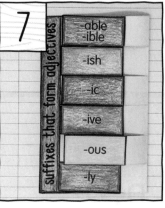

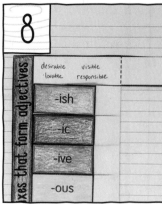

Answer Key:

Noun Formers

-ance/-ence (state, quality) – resistance, extravagance, acceptance, insurance, maintenance, independence, consequence, existence, ambivalence, confidence

-er/-or/-ian/-ist (person who) – collector, predecessor, surveyor, reporter, traveler, veterinarian, physician, mortician, pianist, colonist

-arium/-orium (place where) – aquarium, auditorium, crematorium, emporium, oceanarium, planetarium, sanitarium, solarium, termitarium, terrarium

-ment (result) – document, abandonment, accomplishment, settlement, improvement, assessment, supplement, parliament, amendment, measurement

-ology/-ologist (study of, person who studies) – psychology, psychologist, anthropology, anthropologist, ecology, ecologist, pathology, pathologist, archaeology, archaeologist

-ness (state, condition) – awareness, forgiveness, consciousness, effectiveness, willingness, seriousness, fondness, weariness, homelessness, preparedness

-phobia/-phobe (fear, someone who fears) – acrophobia, acrophobe, arachnophobia, arachnophobe, claustrophobia, claustrophobe, technophobia, technophobe, xenophobia, xenophobe

Adjective Formers

-able/-ible (can be done) – available, desirable, vulnerable, payable, applicable, plausible, visible, flexible, reversible, edible

-ish (having the character of) – sluggish, feverish, boyish, girlish, snobbish, newish, smallish, devilish, selfish, squeamish

-ic (quality, relation) – generic, economic, chronic, specific, domestic, academic, scientific, electronic, historic, romantic

-ive (having the nature of) – combative, festive, sensitive, cooperative, impressive, primitive, aggressive, intensive, attractive, descriptive

-ous (having the quality of) – adventurous, courageous, ambitious, suspicious, marvelous, outrageous, homogenous, luxurious, hazardous, prestigious

-ly (like) – friendly, costly, lovely, orderly, sickly, manly, prickly, deadly, chilly, curly

Verb and Adverb Formers

-ate/-ify [cause (to be)] – manipulate, amputate, communicate, accommodate, eliminate, intensify, quantify, amplify, classify, modify

-en (cause to become) – lengthen, moisten, sharpen, hasten, weaken, frighten, tighten, soften, awaken, dampen

-ize (cause) – moisturize, materialize, rationalize, publicize, organize, authorize, standardize, scrutinize, optimize, memorize

-ward/-wise (in a direction or manner; with) – homeward, forward, outward, awkward, wayward, leeward, seaward, timewise, clockwise

-ly (in the manner of) – particularly, exactly, directly, normally, equally, increasingly, frequently, currently, originally, occasionally

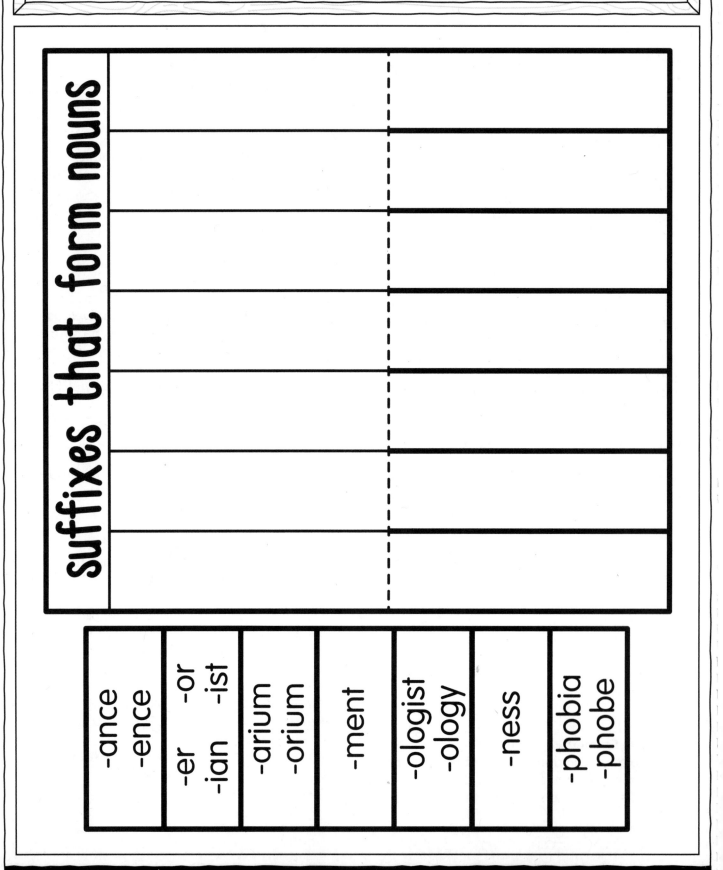

suffixes that form nouns

-ance -ence

-er -or -ian -ist

-arium -orium

-ment

-ologist -ology

-ness

-phobia -phobe

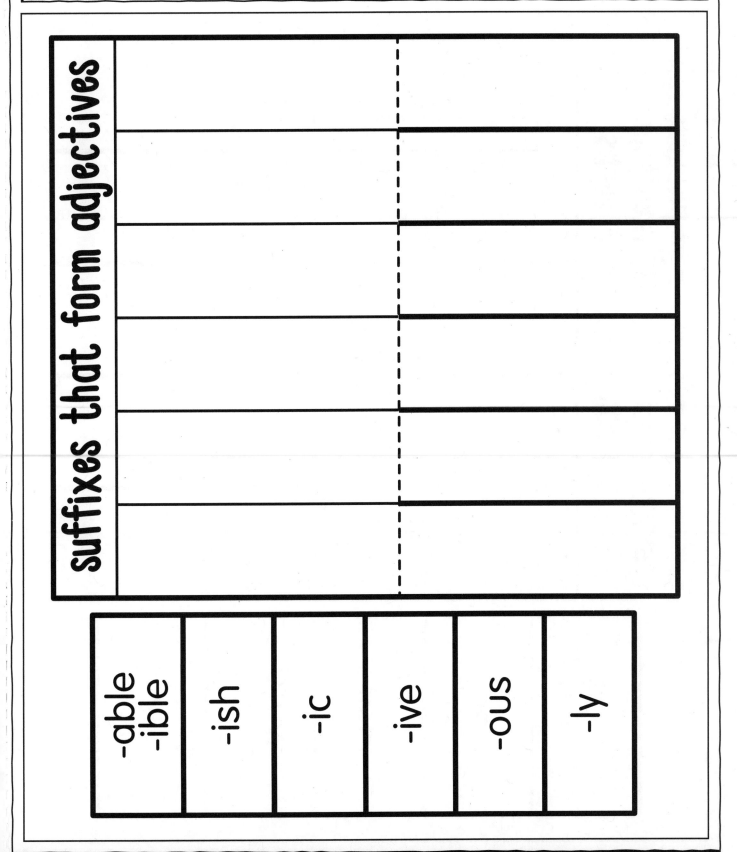

suffixes that form adjectives

-able
-ible

-ish

-ic

-ive

-ous

-ly

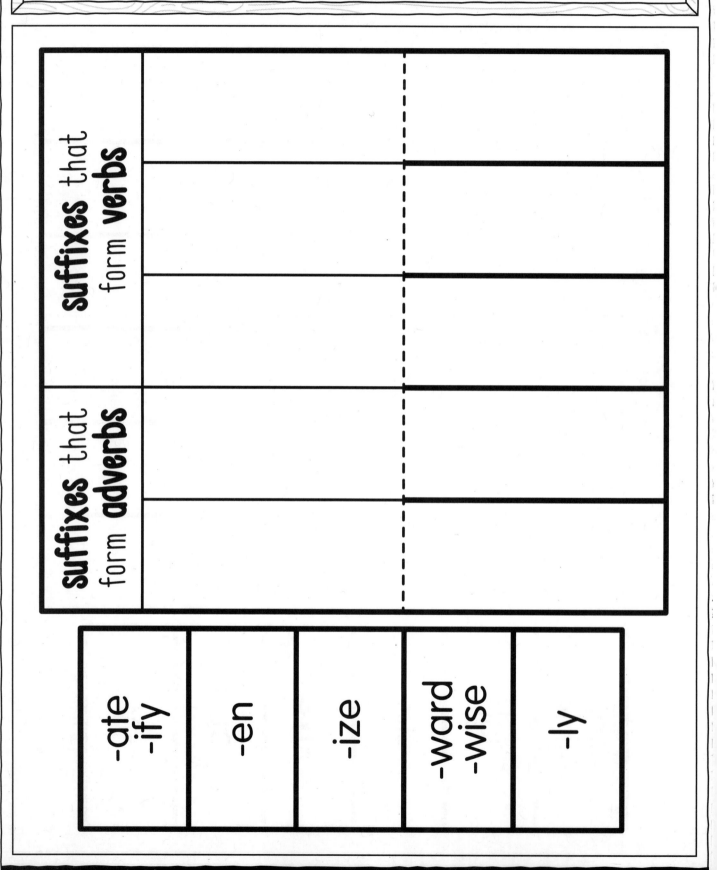

suffixes that form **verbs**

suffixes that form **adverbs**

-ate
-ify

-en

-ize

-ward
-wise

-ly

©2018 Erin Cobb • CD-105003